STARVE
CANCER

and Cook Your Way to a Healthy Lifestyle

STARVE
CANCER

and Cook Your Way to a Healthy Lifestyle

NARGES DARDARIAN

WESTBOW° PRESS

A DIVISION OF THOMAS NELSON & ZONDERVAN

WestBow Press books may be ordered through booksellers or by contacting:

WestBow Press
A Division of Thomas Nelson & Zondervan
1663 Liberty Drive
Bloomington, IN 47403
www.westbowpress.com
1 (866) 928-1240

ISBN: 978-1-4908-2161-0 (e)
ISBN: 978-1-4908-2162-7 (sc)

Library of Congress Control Number: 2014900338

Printed in the United States of America.

WestBow Press rev. date: 1/24/2014

This book is dedicated to the fond memory of my dear father,
Reza Moghaddam, who lost his battle with cancer in April 2006.

Contents

Introduction

In April 2004, during my self-examination, I found a small lump in my left breast. I immediately called my family physician and made an appointment to see him. After examining me, he referred me to a surgeon. I had a biopsy done at the hospital in April, followed by a lumpectomy in June. From the time that the lump was removed until the results were known was a difficult time in my life. I had to wait two long weeks until the results came back, and it was torture. During those weeks, I was so anxious about my results that I made multiple calls to the surgeon's office, but each time, the secretary said that the results were not yet received.

Finally, the surgeon's secretary called and gave me an appointment to see the surgeon. I pleaded with her to give me the result over the phone, but she told me that I had to see the doctor.

My appointment was the following day. I remember thinking while I was driving to his office that I did not have a history of cancer in my family, I had nursed my two daughters, I ate healthy, I did not smoke or drink, and I exercised on an almost daily basis. I assumed that the surgeon was going to tell me that I was fine and that I had fatty tissue and there was nothing to worry about. With this attitude, I went to his office.

When I saw the surgeon, he looked sad, and he told me that the lab results were back and the results were positive; the lump that he had removed was cancerous. I could not believe my ears. Why me? I did everything right. Why was this happening to me?

My surgeon referred me to an oncologist, and from there, I went through a series of X-rays, tests, and lymph-node removal.

My tumor was a grade-one, tubular, ER, PR positive, node negative. I was given sixteen sessions of radiation.

In October 2005, I was cancer free and thought that this was the end of it. I saw my oncologist every six months, and all of the results were positive. I had last seen her in August 2007.

In September 2007, I started coughing and went to my new family doctor, as my previous family doctor had retired. My doctor told me that I had pneumonia. I had three chest X-rays performed, and each time my doctor told me that I had walking pneumonia. I was repeatedly prescribed antibiotic medication. From September until December, the coughing was extreme to the point that I thought that I had fractured my ribs. I knew something was wrong, but I never related my 2004 breast cancer to my current symptoms.

Ladies, take charge of your body. If you have had cancer before or if something is wrong and will not go away, ask to see a specialist.

I was uneducated and did not realize that breast cancer could metastasize to other parts of my body. If you have persistent symptoms that do not go away after one or two weeks of treatment, demand that your family physician refer you to a specialist.

Back to my story ... After three chest X-rays and a variety of antibiotic medication, and suffering with pain in my back and ribs for three months, on December 17, 2007, my family doctor said, "I am sorry your breast cancer is back and has spread to your lungs, ribs, back, liver, and bones."

I was speechless, as I had told my doctor for three months that something was wrong, and she kept treating me with antibiotics for walking pneumonia. She is no longer my family physician.

During this time, I also found another lump in my right breast. I made an appointment with my oncologist and went through six months of intensive chemotherapy treatment, numerous CT scan studies, and a barrage of other tests that I do not even recall.

It was the hardest journey I have ever taken. I gained weight, lost all of my hair, and looked completely different. I could not walk or do normal everyday tasks. I was depressed and tired. But I decided to fight back. With the support of my husband, two daughters, extended family and friends, and a strong will to survive, I am here. I have taken a new approach to life, educated myself, researched, and come up with a healthy diet for myself. It's a diet free of sugar, red meat, dairy, and other harmful products. I am not going to give up. I have too much to live for.

Because of this journey, I have written a cookbook of healthy recipes. *Starve Cancer and Cook Your Way to a Healthy Lifestyle* is a collection of recipes that I developed to help the millions of women living with breast cancer, like me. It focuses on removing alcohol, caffeine, canned products, dairy, red meat, and added sugar from your meals, while helping you in maintaining a delicious and balanced diet. However, this cookbook isn't just for people suffering from cancer. It's also beneficial for anyone who simply wants a healthier diet.

When I set out to write this cookbook, my goal was to eliminate all of the unnecessary and harmful products in our everyday diets. I also recommend that you use organic fruits and vegetables, as well as free-range poultry. Believe it or not, you can sacrifice these ingredients without sacrificing flavor.

Starve Cancer and Cook Your Way to a Healthy Lifestyle includes recipes for a variety of delicious appetizers, soups, salads, entrees, and desserts. They are all easy to follow and take very little time to prepare. A portion of the proceeds from this cookbook will go to breast cancer research.

Some Health Benefits

Almonds: Almonds have an extremely high nutritive value since they contain copper, iron, and vitamins. Almonds also have antioxidant properties.

Asparagus: Asparagus is high in vitamin K and helps detoxify your body.

Avocado: Inflammation is considered the basis of most non-contagious diseases. Avocados have been discovered as anti-inflammatory agents.

Beets: Beetroot fiber has been shown to increase the level of antioxidant enzymes in the body, as well as increase the number of white blood cells, which are responsible for detecting and eliminating abnormal cells.

Cabbage: Cabbage contains phytonutrients and works to protect the body from free radicals that can damage the cell membranes.

Cauliflower: Cauliflower contains selenium and vitamin C, which work together to strengthen the immune system.

Cardamom seed: Cardamom seed helps the body eliminate waste trough the kidneys.

Cayenne pepper: Cayenne pepper contains capsaicin, known to be a powerful antioxidant.

Celery: Celery is anti-inflammatory.

Chickpeas: Chickpeas are a good source of protein. Chickpeas are an excellent source of the trace mineral manganese, which is an essential cofactor in a number of enzymes important in energy production and antioxidant defenses.

Cinnamon: Cinnamon spice contains anti-inflammatory compounds that can be useful in reducing pain and inflammation.

Coconut oil: Coconut oil is good for the immune system. It strengthens the immune system.

Eggplant: Eggplant is rich in antioxidants.

Garlic: Garlic aids in reducing the production of carcinogenic compounds.

Ginger: Ginger root contains a very high level of antioxidants. Ginger can reduce nausea and vomiting and it is anti-inflammatory.

Kale: Kale is high in vitamins K and C and the mineral iron. Kale is a great detox food, filled with fiber and sulfur, which are great for detoxifying your body and keeping your liver healthy.

Leek: Leek contains significant amounts of antioxidants.

Okra: Okra facilitates the propagation of good bacteria referred to as probiotics.

Parsley: Parsley contains volatile oils that are known to neutralize carcinogens, including those found in cigarette smoke and charcoal grill smoke.

Pomegranate: Pomegranate is a powerful antioxidant.

Quinoa: Quinoa is rich in magnesium, which helps body temperature regulation, detoxification, and energy production, to name a few traits.

Spinach: Spinach's vitamins C and E, along with beta-carotene, manganese, zinc, and selenium, serve as powerful antioxidants.

Walnut: Walnut is a good source of all important omega-3 fatty acids.

Zucchini: Zucchini contains vitamin C, which is a powerful antioxidant, and has anti-inflammatory properties.

SOUPS

Barley Soup

2	chicken breasts (skinless, boneless) cut into small pieces
1 cup	barley
1 bunch each	(chives, parsley, dill, spinach, and coriander), chopped
1 cup	chickpeas
1 cup	kidney beans
1 cup	lentil
8 cups	chicken broth
½ cup	rice
2	large onions, chopped
¼ cup	vegetable oil
1 tbsp.	turmeric
½ tsp.	black pepper, freshly grated
½ tsp.	sea salt

1 Wash and soak chickpeas, kidney beans, and lentil overnight and discard water when cooking. Rinse rice and barley separately.

2 Heat oil in a pot, and then add onion and sauté until golden brown. Add chicken, chickpeas, kidney beans, and lentil to onion mixture and sauté for a couple of minutes. Add turmeric and chicken broth to onion mixture and bring to a boil. Then reduce the heat and let it simmer with the lid partially open.

3 When the chickpeas, kidney beans, and lentil are almost cooked, add rice and barley to mixture.

4 When the rice and barley are cooked, add the chopped chives, parsley, dill, spinach, coriander, salt, and pepper to mixture and let it simmer for 10 minutes.

5 Then remove from heat and let the soup cool slightly. Puree the soup in small batches, in a food processor or blender, until smooth.

6 Return soup to the pot and heat thoroughly. You can garnish with caramelized onion.

Serves 8.

Beet and Leek Soup

1   Heat oil in a pot, and then add onion and sauté until golden brown. Add leeks to onion mixture and sauté until wilted. Then add beets, sea salt, peppers, chicken broth, and water to onion mixture. Bring to a boil, then reduce the heat and let it simmer for 30 minutes.

2   Puree soup in small batches in a food processor or blender until smooth. Return soup to the pot and heat thoroughly. You can garnish with chopped chives.

Serves 4.

4 cups	leeks, chopped
3 cups	beets (cooked, peeled, and chopped)
4 cups	chicken broth
4 cups	water
1	large onion, chopped
½ tsp.	sea salt
½ tsp.	black pepper
¼ tsp.	cayenne pepper
⅓ cup	vegetable oil
¼ cup	chives, chopped

Black Turtle Bean Soup

½ cup	black turtle beans
½ cup	green split peas
½ cup	rice
10 cups	chicken broth
1	onion, chopped
2 cloves	garlic, chopped
½ cup each	cilantro and chives, chopped
½ cup	beets (grated with large side of grater)
½ cup	white turnip (grated with large side of grater)
⅓ cup	vegetable oil
1 tbsp.	tarragon, chopped
1	lemon, juiced
½ tsp.	turmeric
¾ tsp.	sea salt
1 tsp.	black pepper

1 Wash black turtle beans and green split peas and soak in water overnight.

2 Heat oil in a pot, and then add onion and garlic and sauté until golden brown.

3 Add turmeric, turtle beans, and green peas to onion mixture and sauté for a couple of minutes.

4 Pour chicken broth and let it cook on medium heat.

5 When beans and peas are cooked, add rice, cilantro, chives, turnip, beets, tarragon, salt, and pepper to the mixture and let it cook for another 15 to 20 minutes. (Save 1 tbsp. of grated beets for garnishing.)

6 Before serving, add lemon juice and let it simmer for a couple of minutes. Garnish with grated beets.

Serves 4.

Cardamom Pumpkin Soup

1   Heat oil in a pot, and then add onion and garlic and sauté until golden brown. Add chopped pumpkin and turmeric to mixture and continue to sauté for 5 minutes.

2   Pour chicken broth over the mixture and bring mixture to a boil, then reduce heat, cover the pan partially, and let it simmer for 15 minutes or until pumpkin is soft.

3   Remove soup from heat and let it cool slightly.

4   Puree mixture in a blender or food processor until smooth.

5   Return mixture to the pot and heat thoroughly, then add cardamom, salt, and pepper.

6   Pour soup into warmed bowls, garnish with chopped oregano, and serve.

Serves 4 to 6.

1	onion, chopped
1 clove	garlic, chopped (optional)
4 cups	pumpkin, chopped
4 cups	chicken broth
¼ tsp.	cardamom, powder
1 tsp.	sea salt
¼ tsp.	turmeric
½ tsp.	black pepper
¼ cup	vegetable oil
¼ cup	oregano, chopped

Cream of Asparagus and Fennel

1 lb.	asparagus
1 cup	fennel, chopped
1	large onion, chopped
2 cloves	garlic, chopped
1	hot chili pepper, chopped
6 cups	chicken broth
4 tbsp.	vegetable oil
1	carrot, grated (for garnishing)
1 tsp.	salt

1   Break off and discard the ends of asparagus, then wash and chop the remaining stalks.

2   In a pot, heat the oil and sauté onion and garlic for 5 minutes. Add asparagus, fennel, chili pepper, and chicken broth.

3   Cover, bring mixture to a boil, then reduce heat and let it simmer until the asparagus is tender but still holds its shape—about 10 minutes.

4   Puree soup in a blender or food processor until smooth. Return it to the pot. Add the salt.

5   Ladle into warmed soup bowls, and garnish with grated carrot.

Serves 4.

Cream of Broccoli and Yam Soup

1   Heat oil in a pot, and then add onion and sauté until golden brown.

2   Add yams and broccoli, and sauté for 5 minutes. Then add the turmeric, cinnamon, cayenne pepper, and sea salt and sauté for a couple of minutes.

3   Pour chicken broth over mixture and partially cover the pot. Bring mixture to a boil, and then reduce the heat and let it simmer for 20 minutes. Remove soup from the heat and let it cool for 5 minutes.

4   Puree soup in a food processor or blender a few cups at the time. Return the soup to the pot and add rice milk. Heat thoroughly.

5   Pour the soup into warmed bowls, and garnish with chopped parsley.

Serves 6.

2 cups	yams, chopped
6 cups	chicken broth
1	onion, chopped
2 cups	rice milk
4 cups	broccoli, chopped
¼ cup	vegetable oil
1 tbsp.	parsley, chopped (for garnishing)
¼ tsp.	turmeric
¾ tsp.	cinnamon, ground
⅓ tsp.	cayenne pepper
½ tsp.	sea salt

Cream of Carrot and Ginger Soup

6 or 7	medium carrots
1	large onion, chopped
¼ cup	fresh ginger
6 cups	chicken broth
2 tbsp.	parsley, chopped
½ tsp.	salt
½ tsp.	pepper
3 tbsp.	olive oil

1   Heat oil in a pot over medium heat, and then add onion and sauté until golden brown.

2   Peel and slice ginger, and then add to onion mixture and sauté for a couple of minutes.

3   Cut carrots into 1" pieces and add to onion mixture and sauté for 2 or 3 minutes. Add sea salt and pepper to onion mixture and sauté for a couple of minutes.

4   Pour chicken broth over onion mixture and partially cover the pot. Bring mixture to a boil, then reduce the heat and let it simmer for 15 minutes or until carrot is tender.

5   Remove from heat. Puree soup in food processor or blender a few cups at a time.

6   Return soup to the pot and heat thoroughly.

7   Serve soup into warmed bowls, and garnish with chopped parsley.

Serves 6.

Cream of Mushroom and Potato

1 Heat oil in a pot, and then add onion and garlic and sauté until golden brown. Add mushroom and potato to onion mixture and sauté for about 5 minutes.

2 Pour chicken broth over mixture and partially cover the pot. Bring mixture to a boil, then reduce the heat and let it simmer for 20 to 25 minutes until the potato is cooked.

3 Puree soup in a food processor or blender until smooth.

4 Return soup to the pot and heat thoroughly. Season it with salt and pepper.

5 Pour soup into warmed bowls and serve with toasted croutons.

Serves 4 to 6.

2 cups	mushroom, chopped
1 ½ cups	potato, peeled and chopped
1	large onion, chopped
2 cloves	garlic, chopped
½ tsp.	cayenne pepper
½ tsp.	sea salt
6 cups	chicken broth
¼ cup	vegetable oil
½ cup	toasted croutons

Cream of Pumpkin and Leek

3 cups	pumpkin, peeled and chopped
4 cups	leek, chopped
1 cup	green apple, chopped
1	onion, chopped
1 clove	garlic, chopped
6 cups	chicken broth
1 tsp.	cinnamon
½ tsp.	black pepper
1 tsp.	sea salt
⅓ cup	vegetable oil

1 Heat oil in a large pot, and then add onion, garlic, and leek and sauté until wilted.

2 Add chopped pumpkin and apple to onion mixture and sauté for a couple of minutes.

3 Pour chicken broth over the mixture, then add cinnamon and bring to a boil. Reduce the heat, partially cover the pot, and let it simmer for 15 minutes.

4 Remove the pot from the heat and let the soup cool slightly. Puree soup, in small batches, in a food processor or blender until smooth.

5 Return soup to the pot and heat thoroughly. Add salt and pepper. Pour soup in to warmed bowls and serve.

Serves 6.

Green-Pepper Soup

1   Slice green peppers and discard seeds.

2   Heat 4 tbsp. of oil in a pot, and then add onion and sauté until golden brown.

3   Add potatoes, carrots, and turmeric and sauté for a couple of minutes.

4   Pour chicken broth over the mixture and bring to a boil, then reduce the heat and let it simmer for 10 minutes. Add green peppers to onion mixture and let it simmer for another 10 minutes or until carrots and potatoes are soft.

5   Add chopped parsley and oregano to onion mixture.

6   Heat the remaining oil in a small pot. Then add flour and sauté for a couple of minutes and add to onion mixture.

7   Add salt and cayenne pepper to the soup.

8   Let soup simmer for 5 minutes and then serve.

Serves 6.

6 cups	chicken broth
4	green peppers
4	medium carrots, sliced thin
2	medium onions, chopped
2	small potatoes, peeled and slivered
3 tbsp.	fresh parsley and oregano, chopped
2 tbsp.	whole-wheat flour
¼ cup	vegetable oil
½ tsp.	turmeric
½ tsp.	cayenne pepper
½ tsp.	sea salt

Kale Soup

4 cups	kale, chopped
1 cup	carrots, chopped
1 cup	celery, chopped
1 cup	cilantro, chopped
6 cups	chicken broth
1 cup	orzo
1	onion, chopped
1 clove	garlic, chopped
½ tsp.	sea salt
¼ tsp.	cayenne pepper
2	lemons, juiced
6 tbsp.	vegetable oil

1 Heat oil in a pot, and then add onion and garlic and sauté until golden brown. Add carrots and celery and sauté for a couple of minutes.

2 Add kale and cilantro to onion mixture and continue to sauté. Pour chicken broth over mixture. Bring mixture to a boil, reduce the heat, and let it simmer with the lid partially open for 10 minutes.

3 Add orzo and simmer for another 10 minutes. Then add salt, pepper, and lemon juice to soup and let it simmer for another couple of minutes. Remove from the heat and pour into warmed bowl.

Serves 6.

Plum and Spinach Soup

1   Wash black-eyed peas and lentil, and then soak them in water overnight separately.

2   Heat the oil in a large pot, and then add onion and garlic and sauté until golden brown. Add chicken pieces to onion mixture and sauté for 5 minutes. Discard the water from the black-eyed peas and add to chicken mixture. Sauté for a couple of minutes.

3   Add turmeric and chicken broth and bring to a boil. Then reduce the heat and simmer for 15 minutes. Discard the water from the lentils and add to chicken mixture and let it cook. When the peas are cooked, add spinach, chives, and plum to the soup and simmer for 10 minutes. After 10 minutes, remove plum seeds from the soup.

4   Dilute whole-wheat flour in ⅓ cup of cold water and pour into the soup. Season with salt and pepper, simmer for 10 minutes, and serve.

Serves 6.

1	chicken breast without bones and skin, chopped in cubes
2 cups	spinach, chopped
6 cups	chicken broth
1 cup	chives, chopped
1 cup	dried plums soaked in water for 20 minutes (or you can use fresh plum, 2 cups)
½ cup each	black-eyed peas and lentils
1 cup	onions, chopped
2 cloves	garlic, chopped
1 tbsp.	whole-wheat flour
½ tsp.	turmeric
½ tsp.	sea salt
1 tsp.	pepper
⅓ cup	olive oil or vegetable oil
⅓ cup	cold water

Plum Soup

½ cup	barley
½ cup	split peas
1 cup each	chives, parsley, mint, kale, and coriander, chopped
¼ cup	vegetable oil
6 cups	chicken broth
2 cups	fresh plum or 1 cup dried plums
2	medium shallots, chopped
2 cups	pears, peeled and chopped
1 tbsp.	dried mint (ground)
½ tsp.	sea salt
1 tsp.	black pepper

1 Wash and soak barley in water for a couple of hours before cooking.

2 Heat 6 tbsp. of the oil in a pot, and then add chopped shallots and sauté for a couple of minutes. Rinse barley and discard the water and add to shallots and sauté more. Then add split peas and sauté for a couple of more minutes. Pour chicken broth over mixture and bring it to a boil, then reduce the heat and let it simmer for 20 minutes.

3 When the barley and peas are cooked, add chopped chives, parsley, mint, kale, coriander, pears, and plums to mixture and let it simmer for 15 minutes.

4 Discard plum seeds and season with salt and pepper.

5 (If you are using dried plum, soak them in water for a couple of hours before cooking.)

6 For garnishing, heat the remaining oil in a pan and add ground mint and sauté for a minute.

7 Pour soup into warmed bowls, and garnish with sautéed mint.

Serves 4.

Pomegranate Soup

1   Heat 4 tbsp. of oil in a large pot, and then add chopped onion and garlic and sauté until golden brown. Add split peas, rice, and chicken broth to onion mixture. Bring to a boil, and then reduce the heat. Cover and let it simmer for 15 minutes.

2   Combine turkey, grated onion, ¼ tsp. of sea salt, and ½ tsp. of black pepper in a mixing bowl and make small turkey balls from the mixture. Heat 2 tbsp. of oil in a small pot, add the turkey balls, and sauté until they are light brown all over. Then add turkey balls, salt, pepper, and pomegranate juice to the soup and let it simmer for 5 minutes. Add parsley, chives, and pomegranate paste and let it simmer for 10 more minutes. Add fresh pomegranate before serving. Use the remaining oil to sauté mint for a minute and use for garnishing the soup.

Serves 8.

6 cups	chicken broth
2 cups	pomegranate juice
½ cup	split peas
¾ cup	basmati rice
2	onions, 1 chopped and 1 grated
2 cloves	garlic, chopped
½ cup each	parsley and chives, chopped
1 cup	pomegranate paste
½ lb.	turkey, ground
¾ tsp.	sea salt
1 tsp.	black pepper
½ tsp.	turmeric
1 tsp.	dry mint, crushed
⅓ cup	vegetable oil
1 ½ cups	fresh pomegranate

Pumpkin Soup

4 cups	pumpkin, peeled and chopped
4 cups	chicken broth
2 cups	rice milk
1	onion, chopped
4 tbsp.	oil
1 tsp.	freshly ginger, grated
1 tsp.	cinnamon
½ tsp.	sea salt
½ tsp.	white pepper
½ tsp.	turmeric

1 Heat oil in a pot, and then add onion and pumpkin and sauté for 5 minutes. Add turmeric and cinnamon to onion mixture and sauté for another 5 minutes. Pour chicken broth over mixture and bring to a boil, then reduce the heat and let it simmer for 10 minutes.

2 Warm up rice milk and add to onion mixture and let it simmer for 5 minutes. Remove the soup from the heat and puree soup in a blender or food processor until smooth.

3 Return the soup to the pot, add salt and pepper, and heat thoroughly. Pour the soup into warmed bowls, and garnish with grated ginger.

Serves 6.

Spinach and Split Pea Soup

1   Wash split peas and soak in water for a couple of hours. Discard water prior to cooking.

2   Heat oil in a pot, and then add onion and sauté until light golden brown. Add split peas to onion mixture and sauté for a couple of more minutes. Then add turmeric, ¼ tsp. of salt, ½ tsp. of pepper, and 3 cups of water to onion mixture. Bring to a boil, reduce the heat, and let it simmer for 20 minutes.

3   In a bowl, mix grated onion, ground chicken, and the remaining salt and pepper and make small chicken balls (hazelnut size) out of this mixture. Add them to onion mixture. Let it simmer for 10 minutes.

4   Add chopped spinach to onion mixture, and let it simmer for 5 minutes. Dissolve rice flour in 1 cup of cold water and add to soup. (Stir the soup as you add the rice flour mixture.)

5   Add orange juice and simmer for 10 minutes. Beat eggs well and add it to the soup while stirring. Simmer for 5 minutes. Pour the soup in warmed bowls and serve.

Serves 6.

4 cups	spinach, chopped
½ cup	split peas
¾ tbsp.	rice flour
1 lb.	chicken, ground
½ cup	vegetable oil
2	medium onions, chopped
1	medium onion, grated
2 cups	orange, juiced
4 cups	water
2	eggs
½ tsp.	turmeric
½ tsp.	sea salt
1 tsp.	black pepper

Tomato Soup

½ cup	rice
2 cups	equally chives, parsley, and basil, chopped; save 1 tbsp. basil for garnishing
½ cup	lentils
1	medium onion, chopped
1 clove	garlic, chopped
4 cups	tomatoes, crushed
2 cups	chicken broth
1 tbsp.	tomato paste
4 tbsp.	vegetable oil
½ tsp.	sea salt
½ tsp.	cayenne pepper

1   Heat oil in a pot, and then add onion and garlic and sauté until golden brown. Add rice, lentils, and chicken broth to onion mixture, bring to a boil, and let it simmer for 15 minutes or until lentils are cooked.

2   Add crushed tomatoes, tomato paste, chopped parsley, chives, basil, cayenne pepper, and salt to onion mixture and let it simmer for 15 minutes.

3   Ladle the soup into warmed bowls, and garnish with chopped basil.

Serves 4.

Turkey and Herb Soup

1 Soak chickpeas, black-eyed peas, and lentil separately overnight and discard the water. Rinse before cooking.

2 Heat oil in a pot, and then add onion and garlic and sauté until golden brown.

3 Add turkey breast pieces, chickpeas, black-eyed peas, and turmeric to onion mixture and sauté for a couple of more minutes. Pour water and bring to a boil, then reduce the heat and let it simmer for 20 to 25 minutes or until the peas are cooked. Make sure the lid is partially open.

4 When the peas are cooked, add rice, lentil, and chopped chives, parsley, dill, coriander, and spinach to the mixture. Let it simmer for 15 minutes or until the soup is thickened. Remove from the heat and serve.

Serves 6.

3 cups	equally divided chives, parsley, dill, coriander, and spinach, chopped
1 ½ cups	equally divided chickpeas, black-eyed peas, and lentils
¾ cup	rice
1 lb.	turkey breast (skinned, boned) cut into small pieces
8 cups	water
2	medium onions, chopped
1 clove	garlic, chopped
4 tbsp.	vegetable oil
1 tsp.	turmeric
½ tsp.	sea salt
1 tsp.	black pepper

Vegetable Soup

2	medium onions, chopped
1	red pepper
2	medium turnips, peeled and chopped
1 cup	celery, chopped
1 cup	carrots, chopped
2 cups	cauliflower, chopped
2 cups	new potatoes, chopped
2 cups	kale, chopped
8 cups	chicken broth
¼ cup	oil
½ cup	whole-wheat noodles
½ tsp.	turmeric
½ tsp.	sea salt
1 tsp.	black pepper

1 Cut the pepper into halves and discard the seeds. Chop coarsely.

2 Heat oil in a pot, and then add onion and sauté until golden brown. Add red pepper, celery, carrots, cauliflower, potatoes, turnips, and turmeric to onion mixture and sauté for a couple of more minutes.

3 Pour chicken broth over mixture and bring to a boil, then reduce the heat, cover, and let it simmer for 15 minutes.

4 Add chopped kale, wheat noodles, salt, and pepper to the mixture and let it simmer for 10 minutes.

5 Ladle the soup into warmed bowls and serve with toasted bread.

Serves 6.

Wheat Soup

1   Soak dry peas, beans, and wheat prior to cooking, preferably overnight.

2   Heat 4 tbsp. of oil in a pot, and then add onion and sauté until golden brown.

3   Add turmeric and sauté for a couple of minutes. Discard the water and add chickpeas, lentils, kidney beans, and wheat to onion mixture and sauté for a couple of minutes. Pour chicken broth over the mixture and bring to a boil, then reduce the heat and let it simmer with the lid partially open for 25 to 30 minutes or until the beans and peas are cooked.

4   Add chopped spinach to mixture and let it simmer for 10 minutes.

5   Heat the remaining oil in a separate pot, then add flour and sauté for a couple of minutes. Add this to the soup.

6   Season with salt and pepper, and ladle the soup into warmed bowls and serve.

Serves 6.

4 cups	spinach, chopped
2 cups	equally divided dry chickpeas, lentil, and kidney beans
2	medium onions, chopped
8 cups	chicken broth
½ cup	wheat
6 tbsp.	vegetable oil
1 tbsp.	whole-wheat flour
½ tsp.	turmeric
½ tsp.	sea salt
1 tsp.	black pepper

SALADS

Avocado and Tomato Salad

2	ripe avocados
2	tomatoes
¼ cup	cilantro, chopped
¼ cup	raisins
¼ cup	avocado oil
1	lime, juiced
½	lemon, juiced
½ tsp.	Tabasco sauce
½ tsp.	Dijon mustard
1 tbsp.	mayonnaise
½ tsp.	sea salt

1   Peel avocado, cut in half, and remove seed and skin. Cut each half into 12 pieces.

2   Cut each tomato into 8 pieces.

3   Mix avocado, tomato, cilantro, and raisins in a bowl.

4   In a small bowl, mix avocado oil, lime juice, lemon juice, Tabasco sauce, mustard, mayonnaise, and sea salt and pour over avocado mixture. Toss well.

Serves 4.

Avocado and Fig Salad

1   Wash and cut avocado in half. Remove the seed and the skin. Cut each half of avocado into a quart and slice.

2   Wash figs and remove the stem, and then cut each 1 into 4 pieces. Slice shallot into rings.

3   Place avocado, figs, shallot, and tarragon in a salad bowl.

4   Mix lime juice, avocado oil, salt, and pepper and pour over the avocado mixture and toss.

Serves 4.

3	ripe avocados
4	large fresh figs
1	small shallot
¼ cup	fresh tarragon, chopped
½ cup	lime, juiced
¼ cup	avocado oil
½ tsp.	sea salt
½ tsp.	black pepper

Cilantro and Quinoa Salad

2 cups	cilantro, chopped
1 cup	quinoa
1 ½ cups	water
½ cup	red pepper, chopped
½ cup	yellow pepper, chopped
½ cup	orange pepper, chopped
½ cup	tomato, chopped
¼ cup	red onion, chopped
½ cup	walnuts, coarsely chopped
¼ cup	fresh lime, juiced
2 tbsp.	olive oil
¼ tsp.	black pepper
¼ tsp.	sea salt

1 Wash quinoa and place in a pot. Cover with water and let it cook on medium heat until the water evaporates and then let it cool off.

2 In a bowl, mix chopped cilantro, peppers, onion, tomato, walnut, and quinoa.

3 In a small bowl, mix olive oil, lime juice, salt, and pepper and pour over the cilantro mixture. Toss.

Serves 4.

Corn and Tuna Salad

1 In a medium pot, bring water to a boil, and then add ½ tsp. of salt and pasta to boiling water and let pasta cook on medium heat for 10 minutes. Drain pasta and let it cool.

2 Drain tuna and place it in a large salad bowl. Break the chunks of tuna with fork. Add celery, green onions, red, orange, and yellow pepper to tuna.

3 When pasta is cold, add it to the tuna mixture and mix gently.

4 In a small bowl, mix lemon juice, olive oil, mayonnaise, ½ tsp. of salt and pepper and pour over salad. Toss well.

Serves 6.

2 cups	whole-kernel corn, cooked
1 cup	solid light tuna
1 cup	small pasta (like alphabets)
2 stalks	celery, chopped
½	red pepper, chopped
½	orange pepper, chopped
2	green onions, chopped
2	lemons, juiced
3 cups	water
3 tbsp.	mayonnaise
¼ cup	olive oil
1 tsp.	sea salt
½ tsp.	black pepper

Mango and Pomegranate Salad

4	yellow mangos
1 cup	pomegranate
1	shallot
2 tbsp.	cilantro, chopped
¼ cup	avocado oil
1 ½	lime, juiced
½ tsp.	Dijon mustard
¾ tsp.	sea salt
½ tsp.	white pepper

1 Remove skin from mangos and take the seed out. Slice each side of mango into approximately 20 pieces and place them in a salad bowl.

2 Cut shallot into rings and add them to mango pieces. Add pomegranate to mango and shallot.

3 Mix avocado oil, lime juice, cilantro, mustard, salt, and pepper in a small bowl and pour over mango mixture.

4 Cover and refrigerate for half hour before serving.

Serves 4.

Mango Salad

1 Peel mangos and take the seed out. Cut mangos into small pieces. Each mango should be cut into 20 pieces. Cut each tomato into 8 pieces.

2 Discard the head of the green onion and chop the onion into small pieces.

3 In a salad bowl, mix mangos, tomato, and green onion.

4 In a small bowl, mix olive oil, lemon juice, sea salt, and pepper and pour over the mango mixture. Toss well and then serve.

Serves 4.

2	yellow mangos
2	tomatoes
1	green onion
¼ cup	parsley, chopped
4 tbsp.	olive oil
1	lemon, juiced
½ tsp.	sea salt
¼ tsp.	black pepper

Medley-Bean Salad

½ cup	red kidney beans
½ cup	black-eyed beans
½ cup	chickpeas
½ cup	black beans
1 cup	chives, chopped
1 cup	parsley, chopped
1	large onion, sliced
1 tbsp.	cumin powder
½ cup	olive oil
⅔ cup	lime, juiced
1 tsp.	sea salt
½ tsp.	black pepper

1 Wash beans and peas and soak them in water the night before.

2 Discard the water and rinse a couple of times. Place beans and peas in a pot and pour enough water to cover the beans and peas. Bring to a boil and then reduce the heat and partially cover the pot. Let it simmer for 35 to 45 minutes.

3 When beans and peas are cooked, drain off the excess water and place in a salad bowl and let it cool off.

4 Add onion, chives, and parsley to the beans and peas.

5 In a small bowl, mix cumin, olive oil, lime juice, salt, and pepper and pour over the bean mixture.

6 Toss gently and serve.

Serves 6.

Pecan, Spinach, and Beet Salad

1 Wash and pat dry baby spinach, then place them in a salad bowl.

2 In a pot, heat 2 tbsp. of grape-seed oil and sauté onion until golden brown. Mix pecans and cayenne pepper with a few drops of water in a bowl, making sure that pecans are covered with cayenne pepper, and then roast them in a pan for 5 minutes. Stir at all times to avoid burning.

3 Peel and cut beets in shoestring shape. Mix onion, pecan, and beets with spinach.

4 Mix the remaining grape-seed oil, Dijon mustard, balsamic vinegar, garlic, and sea salt and pour this mixture over the spinach mixture. Toss and serve.

Serves 4.

4 cups	baby spinach
2	medium beets, cooked
1	onion, sliced
⅓ cup	pecans, pieces
⅓ cup	grape-seed oil
½ tsp.	Dijon mustard
2 tbsp.	balsamic vinegar
½ tsp.	sea salt
¼ tsp.	cayenne pepper
1 clove	garlic, grated

Potato and Corn Salad

2 cups	corn, cooked
2	large potatoes, cooked
2 ½ cups	water
1 cup	pomegranate
½ cup	parsley, chopped
1	lemon, juiced
1 tbsp.	mayonnaise
1 clove	garlic, grated
¼ tsp.	sea salt
Pinch	pepper
4 tbsp.	olive oil

1 Wash potatoes and cook with 2 ½ cups of water in a pot until softened. Then let them cool for 5 minutes. Peel and chop potatoes into small cubes.

2 In a salad bowl, mix potatoes, corn, pomegranate, and parsley.

3 Mix lemon juice, garlic, mayonnaise, olive oil, salt, and pepper.

4 Pour the lemon mixture over potato mixture and toss well.

Serves 4.

Quince and Tomato Salad

1 Cut each quince into half. Remove the seeds and peel them. Cut each half into 4 pieces lengthwise and slice each piece thinly, then place them in a salad bowl.

2 Cut tomatoes into small pieces and add them to quince. Add onion and basil to quince mixture.

3 In a small bowl, mix avocado oil, vinegar, cardamom seed, salt, and pepper and pour over the quince mixture. Toss and serve.

Serves 4.

2	large quinces
2	large tomatoes
1	onion, chopped
½ cup	basil, chopped
¼ cup	avocado oil
2 tbsp.	balsamic vinegar
½ tsp.	cardamom seed
½ tsp.	sea salt
½ tsp.	black pepper

Quinoa and Parsley Salad

1 cup	organic quinoa
1 cup	parsley, chopped
½ cup	green onion, chopped
1 ½ cups	water
1	lemon, juiced
1	tomato, chopped
¼ tsp.	sea salt
¼ tsp.	black pepper
4 tbsp.	olive oil

1 Wash quinoa with water until the water is not cloudy anymore. Then place quinoa with 1½ cups of water in a pot over heat and bring to a boil, then reduce the heat and let it simmer until the water has evaporated. Remove from the heat and let it cool.

2 Mix chopped parsley, onion, tomato, lemon juice, olive oil, salt, and pepper in a bowl, and then add quinoa and mix well.

3 Cover and refrigerate for 30 minutes. Serve and enjoy!

Serves 6.

Shallot and Kale Salad

1   Wash and cut kale leaves into small pieces and place them in a salad bowl.

2   Cut up tomato into small pieces, slice shallot into thin rings, and grate garlic with small side of grater.

3   Add strawberry, mushroom, tomato, and almonds to kale.

4   In a small bowl, mix garlic, avocado oil, vinegar, salt, pepper, and mustard and pour over kale mixture. Toss and serve.

Serves 4.

1 bunch	kale
½ cup	mushroom, sliced
1	tomato
1	small shallot
1 cup	strawberries, sliced
¼ cup	almonds, sliced and roasted
1 clove	garlic
3 tbsp.	fig vinegar
5 tbsp.	avocado oil
½ tsp.	Dijon mustard
½ tsp.	sea salt
½ tsp.	black pepper

Strawberry and Lettuce Salad

1	romaine lettuce
1	carrot
1	tomato
1	cucumber
½ cup	pine nuts
1 cup	strawberries, sliced
1 clove	garlic
2 tbsp.	balsamic vinegar
5 tbsp.	olive oil
½ tsp.	Dijon mustard
½ tsp.	dry mint leaves (ground)
½ tsp.	sea salt

1 Wash and then cut lettuce into small pieces and place them in a salad bowl. Cut tomato into small pieces and add to lettuce. Peel and cut cucumber into thin slices and add to lettuce mixture.

2 Peel and grate carrots with large side of grater and add to lettuce mixture.

3 Place pine nuts in a small pan over medium heat and roast for 5 minutes, stirring all the time to avoid burning. Let it cool for a couple of minutes and then add to lettuce mixture.

4 Grate garlic clove of with small side of the grater

5 In a small bowl, mix garlic, olive oil, balsamic vinegar, salt, mint, and mustard and pour over the lettuce mixture.

Serves 4.

VEGETARIAN

Basmati Rice with Dill

1 cup	basmati rice
1 cup	fresh dill, chopped
1	pita bread
2 tbsp.	olive or vegetable oil
1 ½ tbsp.	sea salt
Pinch	saffron
2 tbsp.	water, boiled

1   Wash basmati rice with cold water 3 or 4 times until the water is not cloudy, then soak in 2 cups of water and salt for a couple of hours prior to cooking.

2   In a pot, bring 3 or 4 cups of water to a boil. Discard the water that the rice was soaked in, pour the rice in the boiling water, then reduce heat and let it boil for 5 minutes. Stir the rice gently to avoid sticking together. When the rice starts floating above the water, add chopped dill. Stir once so dill is mixed with rice, and then drain the rice and dill mixture in a colander.

3   Pour 1 cup of cold water over the rice. This will prevent the rice from sticking together.

4   Heat oil in the pot, and then place pita bread over the oil. Pour rice and dill mixture on top of pita bread.

5   Cover the pot with a paper towel and place the lid over the paper towel. Let the rice simmer on low heat for 20 minutes.

6   Dissolve saffron in 2 tbsp. of boil water and mix it in with 2 tbsp. of rice. Use this as garnish.

Serves 4.

Broccoli Patties

1   Wash broccoli flowers and steam-cook for 10 minutes. Remove from heat and mash it with a fork. Set aside to cool off.

2   Heat 5 tbsp. of oil in a pot, and then add onion and garlic and sauté until golden brown. Remove from the heat and let it cool.

3   In a bowl, beat the eggs for a couple of minutes. Dissolve baking soda in 1 tbsp. of cold water and add it to eggs, then add broccoli, onion, garlic, salt, pepper, and cumin to egg mixture and mix well.

4   Heat the remaining oil in a pan, with a spoon, place the egg mixture into the oil. Make sure they are spaced apart. Cook each side of the patties for a couple of minutes until light golden. Remove patties and place them on a paper towel to remove the excess oil and then serve.

Serves 4.

6 cups	broccoli (flower parts)
4	eggs
1	onion, chopped
1 clove	garlic, chopped
½ cup	vegetable oil
1 tsp.	baking soda
½ tsp.	sea salt
1 tsp.	black pepper
½ tsp.	cumin

Brown Rice with Almonds and Raisins

2 cups	brown rice
1 cup	whole almonds
1 cup	seedless sultana raisins
1	onion, chopped
½	pita bread
1 tsp.	cinnamon
8 tbsp.	vegetable oil
1 tsp.	sea salt

1 Rinse rice 3 or 4 times until the water is clear. Pour enough water over the rice so that it's covered, then add 1 tsp. of salt and let it soak for a couple of hours.

2 In a skillet, roast almonds for 5 minutes and set aside. Heat 4 tbsp. of oil in pot, and then add onion and sauté until golden brown. Add raisins and roasted almonds and sauté for a couple of minutes, then add cinnamon and remove from heat.

3 Boil 4 cups of water, discard the water that was originally in the rice, and add the rice to the boiling water. Reduce heat and simmer. Stir occasionally until rice floats above the water, then remove from heat and pour into a colander. Pour 1 cup of cold water over rice.

4 In a medium pot, heat the remaining oil and place pita bread to cover the bottom of the pot. Pour half of the rice in the pot over the pita bread, and then pour raisin mixture over the rice. Finish pouring the rest of the rice over the raisin mixture. Cover the pot with a paper towel and place the lid over it. Reduce the heat and let it simmer for 10 minutes, and then serve. You can use the pita bread as a garnish; it should be crispy and golden color.

Serves 4.

Couscous with Dill

1   Remove the skin from chicken thighs, wash, and pat dry. Heat oil in a pot, and then add onion and sauté until golden brown. Add chicken thighs to onion and sauté for a couple of minutes; add turmeric, salt, and pepper to onion mixture and sauté for a minute or two.

2   Add water, cover, and bring to a boil, then reduce heat and let it simmer for 30 minutes.

3   Remove chicken and strain the broth. Remove the bones from the chicken thighs and shred the chicken into pieces. Leave this aside.

4   Add couscous to broth and let it cook until the broth evaporates. Just before it evaporates, add dill and mix well. Then add chicken pieces to the couscous mixture. Pour lime juice over the couscous mixture, and garnish it with chopped tomatoes.

Serves 4.

2 ½ cups	couscous
4 cups	water, hot
4	chicken thighs
1 cup	dill, chopped
1	tomato, chopped (for garnishing)
1	onion, chopped
3 tbsp.	vegetable oil
½ cup	fresh lime, juiced
¼ tsp.	turmeric
½ tsp.	sea salt
¼ tsp.	cayenne pepper

Eggplant Quiche

3	medium eggplants
5	eggs
3	medium onions
½ cup	walnuts, chopped
¼ tsp.	saffron
½ tsp.	salt
1 tsp.	pepper
4 tbsp.	vegetable oil

1 Peel eggplants and grate with large side of a grater and set aside.

2 Peel onions and grate them with the small side of grater.

3 Heat oil in a pot, and then add onion and sauté until golden brown. Add eggplant and sauté until the juice has evaporated.

4 Dissolve saffron in 2 tsp. of hot water and add it to the eggplant mixture. Add salt, pepper, and walnuts to eggplant mixture, and then remove from heat and let it cool off.

5 Beat eggs separately and add to the eggplant mixture.

6 Heat oven to 325° F. While the oven is heating up, pour the eggplant mixture in an oiled 9" x 12" oven dish. Place the dish in the middle of the oven and cook for 10 to 15 minutes.

7 Check after 10 minutes and remove if the bottom is light brown. Cut into 12 pieces and turn them over and cook for another 2 minutes.

Serves 4.

Fava Beans and Dill Patties

1 Remove the first and second skin from fava beans, then steam-cook fava beans for 10 minutes. Remove from heat and let it cool off. When fava beans are cold, chop them coarsely.

2 Heat 4 tbsp. of oil in a pot, and then add onion and garlic and sauté until golden brown. Set aside.

3 In a bowl, beat the eggs. Dissolve baking soda in 1 tbsp. of cold water and then add to the eggs. Add dill, sautéed onion and garlic, fava beans, salt, pepper, and saffron to egg mixture and mix well.

4 Heat the remaining oil. With a spoon place the egg mixture one spoon at a time into the oil. (Make sure they are spaced apart.) Cook each side of the patties for a couple of minutes until light golden. Remove patties and place them on a paper towel to remove the excess oil and then serve.

Serves 4.

2 lbs.	fava beans, cooked
1 cup	dill, chopped
4	eggs
1 clove	garlic, chopped
1	onion, chopped
½ tsp.	baking soda
½ tsp.	sea salt
1 tsp.	white pepper
½ cup	vegetable oil
¼ tsp.	saffron

Green-Bean Quiche

1 lb.　green beans
6　eggs
3　medium carrots, cooked
2 tbsp.　whole-wheat flour
2　medium onions
1 tsp.　baking powder
6 tbsp.　vegetable oil
½ tsp.　sea salt
½ tsp.　black pepper
¼ tsp.　saffron

1　Cut off the ends of green beans (drag each end when you cut, in order to get rid of the thread), and then cut each bean diagonally about half an inch long.

2　Peal carrots and slice into small pieces and steam-cook carrots and beans until soft.

3　Chop onions into small pieces. Heat 5 tbsp. of oil in a pot, and then add onion and sauté until golden brown.

4　When carrots and beans are cooked, set them aside to cool a bit.

5　In a large bowl, beat the eggs, and then add to onion mixture. Add flour, baking powder, salt, pepper, saffron, carrots, and beans to onion mixture and mix well.

6　Preheat the oven to 350° F. Oil a 9" x 13" oven dish with the remaining oil. (Make sure the sides are oily as well.)

7　Pour the batter into the dish and flatten with a spoon. Place the dish in the middle rack of the oven and cook for 25 minutes. Cut into squares and serve.

Serves 4.

Kale Omelet

1 Heat oil in a pot, and then add onion and garlic and sauté until golden brown.

2 Add kale to onion mixture and sauté for 5 minutes until soften. Add sea salt and freshly grated pepper and saffron to onion mixture. You can cut this mixture into 6 pie portions and crack 1 egg on each pie portion and cover the dish for a couple of minutes. Remove from heat and serve.

3 This is a very nutritious breakfast.

Serves 6.

2 medium bunches	kale, chopped
2	onions, chopped
2 cloves	garlic, chopped
¼ cup	vegetable oil
6	eggs
½ tsp.	sea salt
½ tsp.	freshly black pepper, grated
¼ tsp.	saffron

Leek and Cilantro Quiche

1 bunch	cilantro
3 stalks	leeks
6	eggs
½ tsp.	sea salt
½ tsp.	cayenne pepper
2 tsp.	whole-wheat flour
1 tsp.	baking powder
½ cup	walnuts, chopped
¼ tsp.	saffron
4 tbsp.	vegetable oil

1 Preheat oven to 350° F., and oil an 8" inch round oven dish.

2 Cut the head of leek and separate each leaf. Wash the leek and cilantro well.

3 Chop leek and cilantro into fine pieces.

4 In a large bowl, mix leek and cilantro.

5 Beat the eggs in a bowl. Add salt, pepper, saffron, flour, and walnuts to egg mixture. Pour this over leek mixture and mix them well.

6 Pour this mixture into the oven dish and place the dish in middle rack. Let it cook for 10 minutes.

7 Remove the dish from the oven after 10 minutes and cut into 12 pieces. Gently turn each portion on the other side to let it cook for another 5 minutes. Both sides should be golden brown.

Serves 4.

Potato and Carrot Patties

1   Place potatoes and carrots in a pot over heat and cover with water. Bring to a boil and reduce the heat, and let it simmer until cooked. Drain the excess water and let it cool for 5 minutes. Remove the skin and mash the potatoes and carrots together.

2   Heat 5 tbsp. of oil in a pot, and then add onion and sauté until golden brown. In a bowl, beat the eggs, then add salt, pepper, sautéed onion, and mashed potatoes mixture to the eggs. Heat the remaining oil in a pan, and with a spoon, place potato mixture one spoon at a time in the pan. Make sure there is a space between them. Cook for a couple of minutes on each side until they have a light golden color. Place the patties on a paper towel to catch the excess oil and then serve.

Serves 4.

2	large potatoes
2	large carrots
1	large onion
2	eggs
¼ cup	olive oil
½ tsp.	sea salt
½ tsp.	pepper, freshly grated

Pumpkin Patties

4 cups	pumpkin, peeled and grated
4	eggs
2	onions, chopped
1 tsp.	cinnamon
½ tsp.	sea salt
1 tsp.	white pepper
¼ cup	vegetable oil

1   Heat 5 tbsp. of oil in a pot, then add onion and sauté until golden brown and set aside.

2   In a bowl, beat eggs until white. Add grated pumpkin, sautéed onion, cinnamon, salt, and pepper and mix.

3   Heat the remaining oil in a pan. With a spoon, place the pumpkin mixture one spoon at a time into the oil. Make sure they are spaced apart. Cook each side of the patties for a couple of minutes until they are a light golden color. Remove patties and place them on a paper towel to catch the excess oil and then serve.

Serves 4.

Quinoa with Tomato and Broccoli

1 Wash tomatoes and place them in a bowl. Pour boiling water over tomatoes and leave for 5 minutes. The skin of the tomatoes should come off easy. Then chop into small pieces and set aside.

2 Rinse quinoa 2 or 3 times. Place in a pot and add water and chopped tomatoes to quinoa. Bring to a boil and then reduce heat and let it simmer for 10 minutes.

3 Chop broccoli flower into small pieces. Then add broccoli, garlic, basil, oil, salt, and pepper to quinoa mixture and let it simmer until the liquid evaporates.

4 This is a great and healthy side dish.

Serves 4.

1 cup	quinoa
1 ½ cups	tomatoes, crushed (2 large tomatoes)
1 cup	broccoli flower, chopped
½ cup	water
¾ tsp.	sea salt
1 tsp.	dry basil or 2 tbsp. fresh basil, chopped
3 tbsp.	avocado oil
1 clove	garlic, chopped
1 tsp.	black pepper
1 cup	water

Sour Cherry Omelet

1 cup	sour cherry, pitted
½ cup	dates, chopped
8 tbsp.	vegetable oil
3 tbsp.	onion, chopped
2	eggs
¼ cup	pistachios, slivered
¼ tsp.	sea salt
¼ tsp.	freshly ground black pepper
Pinch	saffron

1 Heat 4 tbsp. of the oil over medium heat in a pot, and then add onion and sauté until golden brown.

2 Add sour cherries and dates to onion mixture and sauté until the juice has evaporated, then set aside.

3 Beat the eggs well, and then add saffron, salt, pepper, and pistachios. Combine the egg mixture with sour cherry mixture.

4 In a small pan, heat the remaining oil. Using a flower-shaped cutter. Place the cutter in the pan, then pour the egg mixture into the cutter and let it cook for a couple of minutes. Serve with your favorite bread.

Serves 2.

Stuffed Potatoes

1 Peel potatoes and cut a circle on the top. Remove top and then empty the inside, making sure you do not make a hole in the potatoes. Chop the inside of potatoes and set them aside.

2 Chop egg coarsely and place in a bowl. Add chopped parsley, salt, and pepper to chopped egg.

3 In a pot, heat 5 tbsp. of oil and lightly golden-brown all the sides of the potatoes (couple of minutes each side). Remove potatoes and place them on a paper towel to catch excess oil.

4 Heat 3 tbsp. of oil and sauté onions until golden brown. Add inside potatoes and sauté for a couple of minutes. Add 1 cup of tomato juice, tomato paste, and egg mixture to onion mixture and then remove from heat. Fill each potato with egg mixture and place potato top on.

5 Place potatoes on an oven dish. Mix the remaining oil and ¼ cup of tomato juice and pour over each potato. Cook in a preheated 350° F. oven for 20 minutes. Garnish with sprig of parsley, and serve.

Serves 4.

6	large potatoes (same size)
2	onions, chopped
3	eggs, hard-boiled
½ cup	parsley, chopped
1 ¼ cups	tomato juice
1 tbsp.	tomato paste
¼ cup	grape-seed oil
½ tsp.	sea salt
1 tsp.	black pepper

Tarragon Rotini

1 Box	organic whole-wheat rotini (375 g)
3 cups	fresh tomato, chopped
1	tomato, sliced
2 cloves	garlic
½ cup	fresh tarragon, chopped
6 tbsp.	virgin olive oil
1	medium yellow bell pepper
1 tsp.	sea salt
½ tsp.	black pepper
1	lemon, juiced

1 Discard the seeds and stem, and then chop yellow pepper into small diamond shapes.

2 Grate garlic cloves. In a pot, heat oil and sauté garlic until golden brown.

3 Add tomatoes, tarragon, yellow pepper, salt, and pepper to garlic mixture and sauté for a couple of minutes. Reduce heat, and then add rotini to mixture and cover. Let it simmer on low for 20 minutes or until pasta is cooked.

4 Before serving, add sliced tomato and lemon juice and toss.

5 This is a great healthy side dish.

Serves 4.

Vegetable Quiche

1 Chop cranberries into small pieces.

2 In a bowl, mix the chopped parsley, dill, coriander, lettuce, chives, cranberries, walnuts, baking powder, flour, salt, and pepper.

3 In another bowl, beat the eggs and add the parsley mixture, making sure it is mixed.

4 Heat the oven to 325° F. and grease a 9" x 12" oven dish with vegetable oil. Pour in the parsley mixture and smooth the top with a spoon so it is even. Cook for 10 minutes in the middle of the oven.

5 Cut into 12 pieces and turn each piece over. Then place it back in the oven for another 5 minutes.

Serves 4.

½ cup each	parsley, dill, and coriander, chopped
1 cup	chives, chopped
4 leaves	romaine lettuce, chopped
4 or 5	eggs
1 tbsp.	organic cranberries
2 tbsp.	walnuts, chopped
1 tbsp.	whole-wheat flour
1 tsp.	baking powder
½ tsp.	salt
1 tsp.	pepper
4 tbsp.	vegetable oil

Zucchini Quiche

4 or 5 medium zucchini
2 medium carrots, peeled
4 or 5 eggs
3 medium onions, chopped
¼ tsp. saffron
½ tsp. salt
1 tsp. pepper
4 tbsp. vegetable oil

1 Wash zucchini and carrots and discard the ends. Grate them with the large side of a grater.

2 In a pot, heat the oil and sauté onion until golden brown. Add zucchini and carrots and sauté until the juice of the zucchini has evaporated.

3 Dissolve saffron in 2 tbsp. of boiling water. Add saffron, salt, and pepper to the zucchini mixture.

4 Remove from heat and let it cool off completely.

5 Beat the eggs separately in a bowl, and when zucchini mixture is cooled off, add it to the eggs.

6 Heat the oven to 325° F. and grease a 9" x 12" oven dish. Pour the zucchini mixture in the dish and place the dish on the middle rack of the oven. Let it cook for 10 minutes. Check the bottom, and it should be light brown.

7 Cut into 12 pieces and turn each piece over and cook for another 5 minutes.

8 You can serve this as a side or main dish.

Serves 4

POULTRY

Chicken Breast Cutlet

4	chicken breast halves (boneless and skinless)
1 cup	mushroom, sliced
1	onion, chopped
½ tsp.	sea salt
1 tsp.	dry rosemary
½ tsp.	dry ginger powder
¼ tsp.	cumin powder
¼ tsp.	black pepper
½ tsp.	garlic powder
½ cup	bread crumbs
Pinch	saffron
1	egg
½ cup	vegetable oil

1 Wash chicken breasts and pat dry. Slice each chicken breast lengthwise and then again into 2.

2 In a large saucepan, heat oil on medium heat and sauté onion until golden brown. Add mushroom and sauté for a couple of minutes. Set this aside for later.

3 In a flat dish, combine salt, pepper, rosemary, ginger, cumin, garlic, saffron, and bread crumbs.

4 In a small bowl, beat the egg well. Place chicken pieces in the egg and then in bread-crumb mixture. Make sure the chicken breast is covered with bread crumbs all over.

5 In a large saucepan, heat the oil on low and place the chicken inside, letting them cook for a few minutes on each side until golden. Insert a fork in the chicken. If the juice comes out clear, the chicken is cooked. Remove from heat, and garnish with sautéed mushrooms and onions.

Serves 4.

Chicken Kebab with Peanut Sauce

1 In a small dish, mix cumin, onion, coriander seeds, lemon zest, sea salt, pepper, and olive oil.

2 Marinate chicken pieces in the above mixture and refrigerate for a couple of hours.

3 Using a shish-kebab stick, skewer chicken and cook on the barbeque for 2 minutes on each side, or you can cook it in a saucepan with olive oil on the stove until golden brown.

4 Mix ingredients for peanut sauce in a blender. Pour over chicken kebabs and serve.

Serves 4.

1 lb.	chicken breast fillet (cut lengthwise 1" in diameter)
1 tsp.	cumin powder
1	onion, grated
2 tsp.	coriander seeds
1 tsp.	lemon zest
½ tsp.	sea salt
⅓ tsp.	red pepper flakes
¼ cup	olive oil

Peanut Sauce

½ cup	organic peanut butter
¾ cup	organic rice milk
1 tsp.	Tabasco sauce
2 tbsp.	lemon juice
1 tbsp.	tomato paste
½ tsp.	black pepper

Chicken Pizza

Dough

1 pkg.	Fleischmann's instant yeast
2 cups	organic whole-wheat flour
1 cup	water, lukewarm
½ cup	olive oil
1 tsp.	salt

1 In a bowl, mix yeast and lukewarm water and let it sit for 5 minutes.

2 Add olive oil and salt to yeast mixture.

3 Mix flour with yeast mixture slowly and knead the dough until it is not stuck to your hand. (Add more water if you need, cover with towel, and leave for 30 minutes.

Toppings

1 cup	cooked chicken, chopped
3	large white mushrooms, sliced
2	medium tomatoes, sliced
2	shallots, sliced
½ cup	green olives, sliced
⅓ cup	pickled hot pepper rings
Few sprigs	fresh cilantro

1 Mix the ingredients to make the pizza sauce.

2 Preheat oven to 400 F. Oil a 17" x 11" pizza tray. Spread flour on a flat surface and open dough to fit the pizza tray. Make a few holes with a fork on the dough.

3 Pour pizza sauce all over the dough. Spread tomato slices, mushrooms, shallots, green olives, chicken, and pickled pepper rings.

4 Spread cilantro sprigs on top and bake in the middle rack for 20 minutes.

Makes 12 slices.

Sauce

3 tbsp.	tomato paste
1 tbsp.	dry basil leaves
1 clove	garlic, grated
½ tsp.	sea salt
½ tsp.	black pepper
3 tbsp.	olive oil
⅓ cup	water, lukewarm

Chicken Tarragon

1   Wash and pat dry chicken breasts.

2   In a bowl, mix garlic, tarragon, sesame seeds, sea salt, pepper, saffron, and olive oil. Rub this mixture all over the chicken breasts and then place the chicken breasts into bread crumbs, making sure the entire chicken breasts are covered with bread crumbs.

3   Grease an oven dish with olive oil and place chicken breasts on the oven dish.

4   Heat the oven to 350° F.

5   Cook chicken for 30 minutes, turning them halfway.

Serves 4.

2	chicken breasts cut in half (skinless and boneless)
1 tbsp.	dry tarragon leaves or ½ cup fresh tarragon, chopped
1 tbsp.	sesame seeds
2 cloves	garlic, grated
½ tsp.	sea salt
½ tsp.	pepper
2 tbsp.	olive oil
½ cup	bread crumbs
Pinch	saffron

Chicken, Almond, and Wild Rice

2	chicken breasts cut in half (skinless and boneless)
2	medium carrots, peeled and thinly sliced
1	medium onion, chopped
2 cloves	garlic, sliced
3 cups	water
1 cup	wild rice
½ cup	whole almonds
4 tbsp.	vegetable oil
2 tbsp.	pomegranate paste
½ tsp.	turmeric
1 cup	organic raisins
½ tsp.	sea salt
½ tsp.	pepper

1 In a large pot, heat the oil and sauté onion and garlic until golden brown.

2 Add chicken breasts and turmeric to onion and garlic and sauté for a couple of minutes.

3 Pour 2 cups of water over chicken and bring to a boil. Reduce heat and let it simmer for 20 minutes. When chicken is cooked, remove from heat, shred into pieces, and return it to the pot.

4 Add rice, carrots, and 1 cup of water to chicken and let it simmer for 10 minutes. Then add pomegranate paste, almonds, raisins, salt, and pepper to chicken and mix well. Reduce the heat to and let it simmer until the liquid has evaporated and then serve.

Serves 4.

Chicken-Cinnamon Lentils

1   Wash the chicken breast and pat dry.

2   Wash and then soak lentils in water for a couple of hours prior to cooking.

3   In a pot, heat 6 tbsp. of oil and sauté 1 onion until light golden brown, then add chicken and turmeric and sauté for a couple of minutes on each side. Add 2 cups of water to chicken mixture and bring to a boil, then reduce the heat and let it simmer for 30 minutes or until the chicken is cooked. Remove from heat and cut chicken into small pieces and set aside. There should be about a half cup of liquid left. Save this for later.

4   In a small pot, cook lentils with 2 cups of water with partially open lid. Check after 15 minutes to see if lentils are cooked. Drain lentils and set aside.

5   Heat the remaining oil, and then add onion and sauté until golden brown. Add cranberries, lentils, pistachios, cinnamon, salt, pepper, and saffron to onion mixture and sauté for a couple of minutes. Add chicken pieces and the saved liquid to onion mixture and serve over rice.

Serves 4.

1	chicken breast (boneless, skinless)
1 cup	lentils
1 cup	dry cranberries
2	large onions, chopped
½ cup	pistachios, slivered
4 cups	water
1 tbsp.	cinnamon
½ tsp.	turmeric
¾ tsp.	sea salt
½ tsp.	pepper
Pinch	saffron
⅓ cup	vegetable oil

Cranberry Chicken

2	chicken breasts cut in half, skinned and boned
1 cup	lentils
1 cup	dried organic cranberries
1 cup	shallots, chopped
2 cups	water
¼ cup	vegetable oil
½ tsp.	turmeric
1 tbsp.	ground cinnamon
Pinch	saffron
½ tsp.	sea salt
½ tsp.	black pepper
½ cup	almonds, slivered

1 Preheat oven to 350° F. and grease an 8" x 11" oven dish.

2 Wash chicken under cold water and pat dry. Sprinkle lightly with salt and pepper.

3 In a pot, heat 4 tbsp. of oil and sauté both sides of chicken until golden brown. This will take a couple of minutes on each side. Then remove chicken from the pot and set aside.

4 Wash lentils, and cook in a small pot with 2 cups of water for 15 to 20 minutes, or until it is cooked but not mushy. Drain lentils. Keep ½ cup of the liquid and discard the rest. Heat the remaining oil and sauté shallots until golden brown, and then add cranberries and lentil to shallot mixture.

5 Add saffron, turmeric, cinnamon, almonds, and liquid from lentil to shallot mixture.

6 Place the chicken breasts into the oven dish and pour shallot mixture all over. Place the dish in the middle of the oven and cook for 30 minutes.

7 You could serve this dish over quinoa.

Serves 4.

Eggplant and Turkey Quiche

1 Preheat oven to 350° F.

2 Wash eggplants and make a couple of cuts on them, and then place them on an oven dish in the middle rack. Cook for 20 to 25 minutes. Remove from the oven, let it cool, then peel the skin off and chop eggplants into small pieces.

3 In a pot, heat 6 tbsp. of oil and sauté onion and garlic until golden brown and then add ground turkey and sauté until the juice has evaporated.

4 Add turmeric, salt, pepper, saffron, tomato paste, mint, walnuts, and eggplant to onion mixture and sauté for a couple of minutes. Remove from heat and let it cool for 5 minutes.

5 Add eggs 1 by 1 to onion mixture and mix well, then add baking powder and flour.

6 Grease a 9" x 13" oven dish and pour onion mixture; flatten with a spoon.

7 Place the dish in the middle of the oven and cook for 15 to 20 minutes. Cut into squares and serve.

Serves 6.

1 lb.	ground turkey
2	medium eggplants
1	medium onion, chopped
2 cloves	garlic, chopped
6	eggs
1 cup	walnuts, chopped
½ tsp.	turmeric
1 tsp.	baking powder
2 tbsp.	whole-wheat flour
¾ tsp.	sea salt
1 tsp.	black pepper
¼ tsp.	saffron
2 tbsp.	fresh mint, chopped
3 tbsp.	tomato paste
2 tbsp.	whole-wheat flour
½ cup	vegetable oil

Exotic Chicken and Vegetables

2	chicken breasts cut in half (skinless, boneless)
1	large carrot
1	yellow bell pepper
1 cup	snow peas
Juice 2	large oranges
½ cup	organic dry cranberries
2 cloves	garlic
½ tsp.	ground ginger
½ tsp.	ground cumin
½ tsp.	ground cinnamon
½ tsp.	sea salt
¼ tsp.	pepper
Pinch	saffron
2 tbsp.	olive oil

1 Wash and pat dry chicken breasts and then cut into cubes.

2 Mince garlic and rub all over chicken cubes.

3 In a pot, heat olive oil and add chicken cubes and sauté until golden brown (5 to 8 minutes).

4 In a bowl, combine ginger, cumin, cinnamon, saffron, salt, and pepper, and then add orange juice and cranberries.

5 Heat the oven (350° F).

6 Remove chicken cubes and transfer into an oven dish. Pour orange juice mixture all over the chicken cubes and cook for ½ hour.

7 Cut carrots and pepper into 2" strings. Take off the ends of snow peas.

8 Combine vegetables and steam-cook over medium heat for 10 minutes.

9 Remove chicken from the oven and add vegetables. Serve over wild rice.

Serves 4.

Ginger-Pear Chicken Thighs

1   In a pot, heat oil and sauté onion and garlic until golden brown. Add ginger, pears, saffron, salt, and pepper to onion mixture and sauté for a couple of minutes.

2   Remove the skin and wash chicken thighs. With a sharp knife, make a couple of cuts on each thigh.

3   Preheat the oven to 350° F. Grease an oven dish and arrange chicken thighs on the dish. Pour pear juice over chicken thighs and cover the dish with a foil. Cook on the top rack for 20 minutes, and then turn the chicken thighs on the other side and cover them with the pear mixture. Remove the foil, and cook for another 10 minutes.

4   You can serve this dish with vegetables or over basmati rice.

Serves 4.

1	onion, chopped
8	chicken thighs
4 cups	pears, sliced and skinned
1 cup	pear juice
2 cloves	garlic, grated
1 tsp.	fresh ginger, grated
4 tbsp.	olive oil
1 tsp.	sea salt
½ tsp.	white pepper
⅛ tsp.	saffron

Green-Bean Stew

1 lb.	lean ground turkey
1	medium onion, chopped
1 clove	garlic, chopped
3 cups	green beans
4 tbsp.	tomato paste
1 ½ cups	water, boiled
2 tbsp.	vegetable oil
1 tbsp.	cinnamon
½ tsp.	turmeric
½ tsp.	black pepper
1 ½ tsp.	sea salt
Pinch	saffron

1 Cut off the ends of beans by dragging from one end to the other. (This will get rid of the threads on each side of beans.) Wash beans and cut them diagonally about an inch long.

2 In a large, heavy pot, heat oil over medium heat and sauté onion and garlic until golden brown. Add ground turkey and sauté until the juice has evaporated, and then add green beans and sauté for a couple of more minutes.

3 In a small bowl, mix tomato paste, cinnamon, turmeric, saffron, boiled water, salt, and pepper.

4 Pour tomato mixture over the turkey and beans and bring to boil. Cover, and let it simmer for 15 to 20 minutes. You can serve this stew over basmati rice.

Serves 4.

Ground Turkey Tarragon Kufteh

1   In a pot, heat oil and sauté chopped onion until golden brown. Then add ¼ tsp. of sea salt, ¼ tsp. of pepper, turmeric, chicken broth, and lime juice, and let it boil.

2   In another pot, cook split peas in 2 cups of water for 20 to 25 minutes. Drain the excess water and let it cool.

3   In a bowl, mix turkey, herbs, rice, split peas, egg, grated onion, saffron, salt, and pepper, and then roll them into balls the size of a walnut.

4   When onion mixture has boiled, reduce the heat, and with a spoon, gently drop each ball into onion mixture. Let it cook on low heat for 25 minutes. About halfway through, turn the kuftehs (turkey balls) around.

Serves 4.

1 lb.	lean ground turkey
½ cup	yellow split peas, cooked
1 ½ cups	brown rice, cooked
2	onions, 1 chopped and 1 grated
4 cups	chicken broth
½ cup	fresh dill, chopped
½ cup	fresh tarragon, chopped
1	egg
1	lime, juiced
4 tbsp.	vegetable oil
¾ tsp.	sea salt
1 tsp.	pepper
½ tsp.	turmeric
Pinch	saffron

Kale with Tomato Sauce

1 lb.	ground turkey or ground chicken
⅓ cup each	black-eyed peas, lentil, and split peas
2 large bunches	kale (about 20 leaves)
2	onions, grated
⅓ tsp.	sea salt
⅓ tsp.	turmeric
Pinch	saffron
1 tsp.	freshly grated pepper
2 cups	tomato, crushed
½ cup	lime, juiced
3 tbsp.	vegetable oil
2 ½ cups	water

1 Rinse and soak black-eyed peas, lentils, and split peas for a couple hours prior to cooking or over night. Then discard the water and rinse and cook with 2 ½ cups of water in a pot over medium heat. There should be ½ cup of water left after the peas are cooked.

2 In a bowl, mix grated onion, ground turkey or ground chicken, turmeric, saffron, salt, and pepper and make small balls the size of a hazelnut from this mixture.

3 In a pot, heat oil on medium heat and sauté chicken/turkey balls until they are golden brown.

4 Chop kale, then place kale, peas, crushed tomato, lime juice, salt, and pepper, chicken/turkey balls in a pot and cook for 10 minutes with lid closed. You also can serve this dish over wild rice.

Serves 6.

Lasagna

1 In a large pot, bring 12 cups of water to a boil. Add 1 tsp. of salt, and if you are worried about noodles sticking together, add 1 tbsp. of oil. Cook noodles for 10 to 12 minutes. Make sure the water covers the entire noodle. When cooked, drain and pour cold water over the noodles to avoid sticking together.

2 In a pot, heat oil over medium heat until hot, and then add onion and garlic and sauté until golden brown. Then add turkey and continue to sauté until the liquid has evaporated.

3 Add turmeric, saffron, salt, pepper, and chopped parsley to onion mixture.

4 Wash tomatoes and place them in a bowl. Pour boiling water over and let it sit for 5 minutes. Drain water and poke tomatoes with a sharp knife. The skin should come off easily.

5 Chop tomatoes into small pieces, and then mix with tomato paste and pour over onion mixture.

6 Reduce heat and cover. Let it simmer for 10 to 15 minutes. Remove ½ cup of the liquid and set it aside.

7 In a small bowl, beat egg and set aside.

8 Preheat the oven to 350° F.

9 Spread half of the saved liquid on the bottom of a 9" x 13" x 2" baking pan. Top with a layer of noodles, brush the noodles with egg, and then spread sauce over the noodles and top with chopped parsley. Repeat this process, ending with the noodles.

10 Spread the second half of the saved liquid on top of noodles, cover with foil, and bake about 35 to 40 minutes. Let stand 15 minutes, and then cut into serving pieces.

Serves 6 to 8.

12	lasagna noodles, uncooked
1 lb.	extra-lean ground turkey
5	medium tomatoes
1	mediums onion, chopped
1 cup	parsley, chopped
1	egg
1 clove	garlic, chopped
½ cup	tomato paste
1	lime, juiced
¼ cup	olive oil
½ cup	fresh basil, chopped
1 tsp.	sea salt
¼ tsp.	cayenne pepper
¾ tsp.	turmeric
Pinch	saffron

Okra Stew

1 lb.	chicken thighs, boneless, skinless
1	onion, chopped
1 lb.	okra
2 tbsp.	tomato paste
3 tbsp.	lime, juiced
½ tsp.	sea salt
1 tsp.	freshly grated pepper
½ tsp.	turmeric
3 tbsp.	vegetable oil
2 cups	water

1 Wash and remove the ends of okra, then slice each into 5 or 6 pieces.

2 In a pot, heat the oil and sauté onion until golden brown. Cut chicken thighs into quarts and add to onion. Sauté until light golden.

3 Add turmeric, salt, pepper, lime juice, and tomato paste to onion mixture and sauté for a couple of minutes.

4 Add water and bring it to a boil, then reduce heat and let it simmer for 25 minutes. Add okra to onion mixture and cook for another 15 more minutes. Serve over whole-wheat pasta or brown rice or just by itself.

Serves 4.

Orange Duck with Carrots

1   To make slivered orange peel, remove the white part from the skin and cut the skin into half a toothpick size. For 1 cup of orange peel, you need 2 big oranges.

2   In a small pot, boil the orange peel with 1 cup of water on high heat for 5 minutes. Remove from the heat and drain the boiling water. Pour cold water over the orange peel and let it sit for 10 minutes. Peel carrots, and with a food processor or grater, cut them into a toothpick size.

3   In a pot, bring chopped dates with 1 cup of water to a boil. Reduce the heat, and let it simmer until the water has evaporated and it becomes a paste. Set aside to cool.

4   In a pot, heat 5 tbsp. of oil and sauté onion until golden brown. Add duck pieces and turmeric and continue to sauté for a couple of minutes. Add 4 cups of water and bring it to a boil, then reduce heat and let it simmer until the duck is cooked. Cover with the lid partially open while simmering.

5   In a small pot, heat the remaining of the oil and sauté flour for 5 minutes, mixing constantly to avoid burning. Then add orange juice, salt, and pepper to flour mixture and simmer for a couple of minutes. Pour the flour mixture over the duck, and let it simmer for 10 minutes.

6   Mix the carrots, orange skin, date paste, lemon juice, and saffron in a bowl and pour over the duck pieces. Simmer for 5 minutes and then remove from heat.

7   Pour this dish on a serving platter and spread almonds and pistachios on top and serve.

8   You can serve this exotic dish over basmati or wild rice.

Serves 6.

2 lbs.	duck breast (skinless and boneless chopped into cubes)
4	medium carrots
1 cup	orange peel, slivered
2	onions, chopped
3 tbsp.	pistachios, slivered
3 tbsp.	almonds, slivered
½ cup	dates chopped
3 tbsp.	lemon, juiced
5 cups	water
½ cup	olive oil
2 cups	fresh orange, juiced
1 tbsp.	whole-wheat flour
¼ tsp.	saffron
½ tsp.	turmeric
½ tsp.	sea salt
½ tsp.	black pepper

Orange-Pistachio Rice

1 cup	orange peel slivered (2 large oranges)
2 cups	basmati rice
1 tbsp.	freshly grated ginger
1 cup	carrot, grated
1 cup	dates, chopped and pitted
8 tbsp.	vegetable oil
1 cup	pistachios, slivered
½ cup	onion, chopped
1 clove	garlic, chopped
1 tbsp.	cumin seed
⅓	ground nutmeg
¼ tsp.	saffron
¼ tsp.	cayenne pepper
1 tsp.	sea salt
½ cup	chicken broth
4 cups	water

1 Rinse rice 4 or 5 times in cold water to remove excess starch, then cover rice with water and ½ tsp. of salt and allow this mixture to rest for 30 minutes.

2 Cut a circle from the bottom of the orange and divide the orange into 4 quarters. Remove the orange skin and then remove the white part from the orange part. Cut the skin as thin as a match stick and about an inch long. Orange peel is bitter, so to take the bitterness away, place them in a small pot and cover with 1 cup of water and boil for 5 minutes. Then drain and rinse with cold water and set aside.

3 In a pot, heat 4 tbsp. of oil and sauté onion and garlic until golden brown. Add carrots, ginger, dates, cumin, nutmeg, pepper, saffron, and remaining salt and sauté for a couple of minutes. Add chicken broth and let it simmer until the liquid evaporates (a couple of minutes). Add pistachios and orange skin to onion mixture and set aside.

4 Discard water that rice has been soaked in and bring rice and 4 cups of water in a pot to a boil. Add 4 tbsp. of oil and reduce the heat and let it simmer until the water has evaporated with the lid partially open. Combine onion mixture with rice and simmer for 2 minutes with the lid closed. Remove from the heat, fluff with a fork, and serve on a platter.

Serves 6.

Pomegranate and Walnut Stew

1   In a small pan, mix chopped dates and 1 cup of water. Bring it to a boil. Reduce heat and simmer for 5 minutes. (It will look like a paste.) Remove from the heat and set aside to cool.

2   In a pot, heat oil and sauté onion until golden brown. Add chicken breasts and walnuts and sauté for a couple of minutes. Add 4 cups of water, bring to a boil, reduce the heat, and simmer for 30 minutes.

3   When chicken is cooked, remove and share into small pieces. Return it to the pot.

4   Mix pomegranate paste, tomato paste, date paste, saffron, salt, and pepper and pour over the chicken. Simmer on low heat for 30 minutes or until you can see the walnut oil on the surface.

5   You can serve this stew with basmati rice.

Serves 4.

1	chicken breast, boneless and skinless
2 cups	walnuts, finely chopped
2	onions, chopped
1 cup	dates, chopped
2 cups	pomegranate paste
1 tbsp.	tomato paste
4 tbsp.	vegetable oil
½ tsp.	sea salt
½ tsp.	black pepper
¼ tsp.	saffron
5 cups	water

Spinach Turkey Balls

1 lb.	ground turkey
2 cups together	black-eyed peas, split peas, and lentils
1 bunch	spinach
2	onions, chopped
2 cups	turkey or chicken broth
½ cup	grape-seed oil
½ tsp.	sea salt
½ tsp.	turmeric
½ tsp.	dry tarragon
1 tsp.	black pepper

1   Wash and soak peas the night before, then discard water and cook the peas with 3 cups of water on medium heat until it is cooked. Discard the excess water and set aside.

2   Wash and chop spinach. In a pot, heat ¼ cup of oil and sauté 1 onion and chopped spinach for a couple of minutes. Add salt and pepper and continue to sauté for a couple of minutes, then remove from heat and let it cool off.

3   Combine turkey, cooked peas, sautéed onion, and spinach in a bowl and make it into balls the size of a walnut.

4   In a pot, heat the remaining oil and sauté onion until golden brown, and then add turmeric and dry tarragon to onion mixture. Add turkey broth and turkey balls to onion mixture and let it simmer on low heat for 25 minutes.

Serves 4.

Split Peas and Basil Patties

1   In a bowl, pour rice milk over bread crumbs and let it sit.

2   In another bowl, grate the onions.

3   Wash split peas and let it cook with water in a pot over medium heat until soft. Drain after.

4   Add ground turkey, chopped basil, split peas, roasted almonds, eggs, salt, pepper, saffron, and grated onion to bread crumbs and mix well. Make patties from this mixture.

5   In a pan, heat oil and place each patties on the pan. Golden-brown each side. Place patties on paper towels to catch excess oil and serve.

Serves 6.

1 lb.	ground turkey
2	onions
1 cup	split peas
2	eggs
1 cup	basil, chopped
½ cup	almonds, roasted
½ cup	rice milk
1 cup	bread crumbs
½ tsp.	sea salt
½ tsp.	black pepper
¼ tsp.	saffron
¼ cup	vegetable oil
2 cups	water

Stuffed Artichoke

10	artichokes
2 cups	mushroom, chopped
1 cup	almond milk
1 tbsp.	whole-wheat flour
½ cup	grape-seed oil
200 g	ground chicken or turkey
1	onion, chopped
1 tsp.	pepper
1 tsp.	sea salt
2 cups	water

1 Place artichokes in a pot with ½ tsp. of salt and 2 cups of water. Bring to a boil, then reduce heat and let it simmer on low until the artichokes are cooked. When the leaves come off easily, they are cooked. Discard water and let it cool.

2 Take 2 of the artichokes and take off the leaves until you get to the heart of the artichoke. Chop the heart into small pieces, and set aside.

3 In a pot, heat ¼ cup of oil and sauté onion until golden brown. Add ground chicken or turkey and sauté until the liquid evaporates. Add chopped mushroom, artichoke heart, salt, and pepper to onion mixture and set aside.

4 In a pot, heat the remaining oil and sauté flour for 5 minutes, stirring constantly to avoid burning. Add almond milk to flour mixture and bring it to a boil. Reduce heat and let it simmer for a couple of minutes. Remove from heat.

5 Remove the top artichoke leaves, fill each artichoke with turkey or chicken mixture, and place them on an oven dish. Pour almond milk mixture over each artichoke, cover the dish with foil, and bake for 30 minutes in a preheated 350° F. oven.

Serves 4.

Stuffed Chicken Breast

1 Cut chicken breasts open like a butterfly.

2 In a pot, heat half the oil and sauté onion and garlic until golden brown. Remove from heat and add cilantro, ¼ tsp. of salt, ½ tsp. of pepper, and ½ tsp. of nutmeg.

3 Stuff each chicken breast with onion mixture and use a toothpick to keep the chicken breasts together.

4 Mix bread crumbs with salt and pepper and set aside.

5 Beat the egg well and dip each chicken breast in and then transfer them into the bread-crumb mixture, making sure both sides are covered.

6 In a pot, heat the remaining oil and golden-brown each side of the chicken for a couple of minutes.

7 Arrange chicken breasts in an oven dish and pour peach juice all over them.

8 Preheat the oven to 350° F. and place the chicken in the middle rack for 35 to 40 minutes.

9 You can serve the chicken with basmati rice or salad as a side dish.

Serves 4.

2	chicken breasts (boneless, skinless, cut in half)
1	onion, chopped
2 cloves	garlic, chopped
1 cup	cilantro, chopped
½ cup	bread crumbs
2 cups	fresh peach, juiced
1	egg
½ tsp.	sea salt
1 tsp.	white pepper
½ tsp.	nutmeg powder
¼ cup	vegetable oil

Stuffed Eggplant

12	Italian eggplants
1 lb.	lean ground chicken
1 lb.	equally divided chives, parsley, mint, tarragon, and green onion, chopped
½ cup	brown rice
2	medium onions, chopped
1 clove	garlic, chopped
½ cup	vegetable oil
3 tbsp.	tomato paste
1 cup	water
1 cup	lime, juiced
¾ cup	water, boiled
½ tsp.	turmeric
½ tsp.	sea salt
1 tsp.	black pepper
Pinch	saffron

1 With a sharp knife, cut off the eggplant stems and leave ½ inch of the green part on. Remove skin and make a cut lengthwise on 1 side of the eggplant.

2 Wash and spread ½ tsp. of sea salt on the eggplant and let it stand in a strainer for a couple of hours before cooking. (This will get rid of the bitterness of eggplant.)

3 In a pot, bring rice, 1 cup of water, and a pinch of salt to a boil, then reduce heat and let it simmer until the water is evaporated.

4 In a pot, heat 6 tbsp. of oil and sauté onion and garlic until golden brown. Add ground chicken, turmeric, and saffron to onion mixture and sauté until the liquid evaporates (about 5 minutes). Add the herbs and rice to onion mixture and continue to sauté for a couple of minutes.

5 In a bowl, mix 2 tbsp. of tomato paste with ½ cup of warm water, ½ cup of lime juice, salt, and pepper and pour over the onion mixture. Remove from heat and set aside.

6 Preheat oven to 350° F. Oil a pizza tray and place the eggplants on the tray. Place the tray in the middle of the oven. Check every couple of minutes and make sure the eggplants are light brown all over.

7 Remove the eggplants from the oven and place them on a plate over a paper towel to catch the excess oil and let them cool for 10 minutes. (Leave the oven on.)

8 Open gently the cut side of the eggplant and fill each eggplant with the onion mixture. Arrange eggplants with open side up in an oven dish.

9 Mix the rest of tomato paste, lime juice, salt, pepper, and boiled water, and pour over eggplants.

10 Cover with aluminum foil and cook in the middle of the oven for 30 minutes.

11 You can serve this meal over brown rice.

Serves 6.

Stuffed Peppers

1   In a pot, heat 5 tbsp. of oil and sauté onion and garlic until golden brown. Add ground turkey and sauté until the liquid has evaporated.

2   Add green onion, tarragon, parsley, cilantro, rice, and turmeric to onion mixture and sauté for a couple of minutes.

3   In a bowl, mix tomato paste, water, remaining oil, lime juice, salt, and pepper. Pour half of this sauce over the rice mixture and let it simmer for 10 minutes on low heat.

4   Rinse peppers and remove the top. Discard seeds and cut each pepper lengthwise into three.

5   Fill each third of the pepper with the rice mixture and place them on an oven dish. Pour the rest of the sauce over them. Cover the dish with foil and place the dish in a preheated 350° F. oven. Cook for 20 minutes and serve.

Serves 4.

4	peppers (red, orange, yellow, and green)
1 lb.	ground turkey
½ cup each	green onion, tarragon, parsley, and cilantro, chopped
1	onion, chopped
1 clove	garlic, chopped
1 cup	lime, juiced
½ cup	rice, cooked
½ cup	tomato paste
1 cup	water
¼ cup	vegetable oil
½ tsp.	turmeric
½ tsp.	sea salt
1 tsp.	black pepper

Stuffed Quince

6	large quinces
½ lb.	ground turkey
½ cup	rice
1	onion, chopped
1 cup	lemon, juiced
1 cup	water
½ cup	raisins
½ cup	grape-seed oil
1 tbsp.	tomato paste
½ tsp.	sea salt
1 tsp.	black pepper
½ tsp.	turmeric
⅛ tsp.	saffron

1. Cut a circle at the top of each quince and save it for later. With a knife, empty the inside and make sure you do not make a hole on the quince.

2. In a pot, heat 6 tbsp. of oil and sauté onion until golden brown. Add turkey and turmeric and sauté until the liquid evaporates. Add raisins to onion mixture and sauté for a couple of more minutes.

3. In a pot, bring rice and 1 cup of water to a boil, and then reduce the heat and let it simmer until the water evaporates.

4. In a pot, combine ½ cup of lemon juice, tomato paste, salt, and pepper and bring to a boil. Once it's boiled, remove from heat and add saffron, onion mixture, and rice.

5. Stuff each quince with onion mixture and place the tops of the quince back on. Place stuffed quince in a pot. Mix remaining lemon juice and oil and pour over quince. Cover and cook on low heat for 35 to 40 minutes.

Serves 4.

Stuffed Tomatoes

1   Wash tomatoes and cut a circle at the top of each tomato. Remove the circle and empty the inside with a spoon. Make sure you do not make a hole in the tomato. Keep the circles and put them aside. Chop the inside of the tomato and leave it aside.

2   In a pot, heat oil on medium and then add chopped onion and sauté until golden brown. Add turkey and sauté until the juice has evaporated. Add the herbs and sauté for a couple of minutes.

3   Add turmeric, saffron, ½ tsp. of pepper , ½ tsp. of salt, 1 cup of tomato juice, tomato paste, and the inside of the tomatoes to onion mixture. Reduce heat, and with cover partially open, let it simmer for 10 minutes.

4   Wash quinoa and cook with 1 ½ cups of water with open lid until the water evaporates.

5   Mix quinoa, the pine nuts, and onion mixture, and fill each tomato with quinoa mixture. Place tomatos in an oven dish. (Place the tomato tops on each tomato.)

6   In a bowl, mix the remaining tomato juice, lemon juice, salt, and pepper and pour over the stuffed tomatoes. Cover the dish with aluminum foil.

7   Heat the oven to 350° F., and place oven dish in the middle rack and cook stuffed tomatoes for 20 minutes.

Serves 4.

1 lb.	ground turkey
8	medium to large tomatoes
1 cup each	fresh cilantro, chives, and chopped
⅓ cup	fresh mint, chopped (or 1 tbsp. dry mint)
⅓ cup	fresh tarragon, chopped (or 1 tbsp. dry tarragon)
1 cup	quinoa
½ cup	pine nuts
1	onion, chopped
½ cup	vegetable oil
2 cups	fresh tomato, juiced
1 ½ cups	water
2 tbsp.	tomato paste
Pinch	saffron
¼ tsp.	turmeric
1 tsp.	black pepper
1 tsp.	sea salt
½ cup	fresh lemon, juiced

Tomato Chicken Breast

4	chicken breast halves, skinned
4	large tomatoes
½ cup	fresh tarragon, chopped
1	onion, chopped
1 clove	garlic, chopped
¼ cup	virgin olive oil
1 tsp.	sea salt
½ tsp.	black pepper
½ tsp.	turmeric

1   Place tomatoes in a bowl and cover with boiling water. Let it sit for 5 minutes. The skin should come off easily. Discard the skin and chop tomato into small pieces.

2   In a pot, heat oil and sauté onion and garlic until golden brown. Add chopped tomato, tarragon, salt, pepper, and turmeric to onion mixture and let is simmer for 5 minutes.

3   Wash chicken and pat dry. Make a couple of cuts on each piece and place them in an oven dish. Pour onion mixture over the chicken breasts and cover the dish with foil.

4   Preheat the oven to 350° F. Place the dish in the middle of the oven and cook for 30 to 35 minutes.

Serves 4.

Turkey and Potato Loaf

1 Preheat oven to 350° F.

2 Place potatoes in a large pot and cover with water. Boil on medium heat for 20 to 30 minutes or until potatoes are cooked, then drain and let it cool.

3 Remove the skin and then grate potatoes with the large side of the grater. Grate onion and garlic with small side of grater.

4 In a large bowl, beat the eggs. Then mix in potatoes, onion, garlic, turkey, ½ tsp. of salt, ¼ tsp. of pepper, 2 tbsp. of tomato paste, Tabasco sauce, bread crumbs, and chopped parsley together and shape into a loaf.

5 Place the turkey loaf on a greased 9" x 5" x 3" oven dish. Mix 1 tbsp. of tomato sauce with ½ cup of water, the remaining salt and pepper, and pour over the turkey loaf. Cook in the middle rack for 30 minutes.

6 Garnish with chopped parsley and tomato and serve.

Serves 4 to 6.

1 lb.	ground lean turkey
6	small potatoes
1	onion, chopped
1	tomato for garnishing
1 clove	garlic, chopped
1 tsp.	sea salt
½ tsp.	ground black pepper
3 tbsp.	tomato paste
⅓ cup	bread crumbs
⅓ tsp.	Tabasco sauce
½ cup	parsley, chopped (optional)
2	eggs

Turkey Burger with Hazelnut

1 lb.	ground turkey
1	egg
1	onion, grated
2 cloves	garlic, minced
1 cup	hazelnuts, chopped roasted
1 tbsp.	oregano
½ tsp.	sea salt
½ tsp.	black pepper

1 In a large bowl, mix ground turkey, egg, grated onions, minced garlic, roasted hazelnuts, oregano, salt, and pepper. Work with your hands so it is mixed well. Refrigerate for a couple of hours.

2 Make turkey mixture into 4 burgers and barbeque or cook in a pan on the stove for a couple of minutes on each side until cooked. (Use 2 tbsp. of oil if you are cooking on the stove.)

3 Serve with mustard, sliced tomatoes, and pickled cucumbers.

Serves 4.

Turkey Loaf with Eggplant

1   In a pot, heat oil and sauté chopped onion and garlic until golden brown. Add ground turkey and sauté for 5 minutes until liquid has evaporated. Add turmeric, saffron, salt, and pepper to onion mixture and sauté for a couple of minutes. Stir in the pomegranate paste and set aside to cool.

2   In a pot, heat the remaining oil and add grated eggplant, fresh chopped mint, and walnuts. Sauté for a couple of minutes. Let it sit to cool.

3   In a bowl, beat eggs, and then add flour, onion mixture, and eggplant mixture to eggs and shape into a loaf. Place the loaf on a greased 5" X 9" oven dish. Heat oven to 350° F. and cook the turkey loaf in the middle of the oven for 30 to 35 minutes. Garnish with sliced tomatoes.

Serves 4.

1 lb.	lean ground turkey
2	eggplant, skinned and grated (with large side of grater)
1	onion, chopped
2 cloves	garlic, chopped
3	eggs
2 tbsp.	whole-wheat flour
3 tbsp.	pomegranate paste
¼ cup	vegetable oil
½ tsp.	turmeric
1 tsp.	sea salt
1 tsp.	black pepper
¼ tsp.	saffron
2 tbsp.	fresh mint, chopped
1 cup	walnuts, chopped
1	tomato, sliced (for garnishing)

Turkey Loaf with Zucchini

1 lb.	lean ground turkey
2	zucchini, grated
1	onion, chopped
2 cloves	garlic, chopped
1	large carrot, grated
3	eggs
⅓ cup	almonds, slivered
⅓ cup	red currants
¼ cup	vegetable oil
2 tbsp.	whole-wheat flour
½ tsp.	turmeric
½ tsp.	nutmeg, grated
¼ tsp.	saffron
1 tsp.	sea salt
1 tsp.	black pepper

1 In a pot, heat 4 tbsp. of oil and sauté onion and garlic until golden brown. Add ground turkey and sauté until the liquid has evaporated, and then add turmeric, saffron, salt, nutmeg, and pepper. Stir and set aside to cool.

2 In a pot, heat the remaining oil, and then add grated zucchini, carrots, and almonds and sauté for a couple of minutes until the juice has evaporated. Let it sit to cool.

3 In a large bowl, beat eggs. Add flour, currants, onion and zucchini mixture with the eggs. Work with your hands and shape the mixture into a loaf. Place in a greased oven dish.

4 Heat oven to 350° F. and cook the turkey loaf in middle of the oven for 30 to 35 minutes.

Serves 4.

FISH

87

Rainbow Fillet with Tarragon

4 pieces	rainbow trout fillets (1 lb.)
2 tbsp.	fresh tarragon, chopped
2	limes, juiced
2 tbsp.	olive oil
1 clove	garlic, grated
1	onion, sliced into rings
1	small tomato, cut into shape of flower for garnishing
Few sprigs	parsley for garnishing
1	lime cut into quarters for garnishing
½ tsp.	sea salt
1 tsp.	freshly grated black pepper
¼ tsp.	saffron

1 Wash fillets and pat dry.

2 In a bowl, mix lime juice, olive oil, chopped tarragon, garlic, onion rings, salt, pepper, and saffron.

3 Place aluminum foil over an 11" x 13" oven dish and place the rainbow fillets with the skin side down. Pour the lime mixture all over the fish and cover with foil, and then refrigerate for 30 minutes.

4 Preheat oven to 350° F. and place the fish in the middle of the oven. Cook for 20 minutes.

5 Garnish with lime, parsley, and tomato.

Serves 4.

Rainbow Trout with Mushroom

1   In a pot, heat 5 tbsp. of oil and sauté onion until golden brown, then add chopped mushrooms and sauté until the juice has evaporated. Add parsley, chopped almonds, salt, and pepper and sauté for a couple of minutes. Set aside.

2   In another pot, heat the remaining oil and sauté flour until it turns color, stirring constantly to avoid burning. Add almond milk and let it simmer for a couple of minutes until it becomes thick.

3   Wash and pat dry rainbow fillets. Mix cranberry, mustard, and lime juice in a small bowl. Brush each fillet with this mixture. Place 2 tbsp. of mushroom mixture on 1 side and roll up the fillet. Close it with a toothpick.

4   Preheat the oven to 350° F. and place the fillets on a foil-lined baking pan. Pour half of the almond sauce on top of each fillet and cook for 25 minutes. Keep the remaining almond sauce warm.

5   Place the cooked fillet on a serving platter and pour the remaining almond sauce over.

Serves 4.

2 lbs.	rainbow trout fillet, skinned
2 cups	mushroom, chopped
2 cups	almond milk
½ cup	almonds, roasted and chopped
2 tbsp.	flour
1 tsp.	cranberry mustard
1	onion, chopped
¼ cup	grape-seed oil
½ cup	lime, juiced
¼ cup	parsley, chopped
½ tsp.	sea salt
1 tsp.	white pepper

Rosemary Dijon Salmon

2 lbs.	salmon fillet
½ cup	fresh lime, juiced
1 tbsp.	Dijon mustard
½ cup	grape, juiced
1 clove	garlic, grated
½ tsp.	sea salt
⅛ tsp.	cayenne pepper
1 tbsp.	fresh rosemary, chopped
1 tbsp.	fresh ginger, chopped
1 tbsp.	olive oil
Pinch	saffron

1 Preheat oven to 350° F. Wash and pat dry salmon fillet.

2 In a bowl, mix garlic, lime juice, mustard, grape juice, sea salt, pepper, rosemary, olive oil, ginger, and saffron.

3 Place the fillet on a foil-lined baking pan. Pour the garlic mixture all over the salmon fillet and close the sheet loosely. Place the dish in the middle rack and cook for 15 to 20 minutes.

Serves 4.

Shrimp and Mushroom Stew

1 Wash shrimp and drain the excess water.

2 In a large pot, heat the oil and sauté garlic for a couple of minutes. Add the shrimp and sauté until they turn pink. Add sliced mushrooms and sauté for a couple of minutes more.

3 In a small bowl, mix curry powder, flour, sea salt, black pepper, and milk, and pour this mixture over the shrimp mixture. Let it simmer for 10 to 15 minutes until the sauce becomes thick.

4 Serve over basmati rice or whole-wheat pasta.

Serves 4.

1 lb.	shrimp, cooked
2 cups	mushrooms, sliced
1 ½ cups	rice milk
2 cloves	garlic, chopped
½ cup	olive oil
2 tbsp.	curry powder
1 tbsp.	whole-wheat flour
½ tsp.	sea salt
1 tsp.	black pepper

Shrimp with Basmati Rice

1 lb.	baby shrimp, cooked
2 cups	basmati rice
4 cups	water
2 cups	green cabbage, chopped
2 cloves	garlic, chopped
½ cup	fresh tarragon, chopped
½ cup	grape-seed oil
½ tsp.	turmeric
1 tsp.	sea salt
½ cup	lime, juiced
1 tsp.	black pepper
Pinch	saffron

1   In a pot, heat 6 tbsp. of oil and sauté garlic, shrimp, and cabbage until the cabbage is wilted. Add chopped tarragon to garlic mixture and sauté a couple of minutes. Then add turmeric, ¼ tsp. of salt, pepper, saffron, and lime juice and remove from the heat.

2   Rinse rice with water few times and then pour the rice with 4 cups of water and the remaining oil and salt in a pot. Bring to a boil. Reduce heat and cover partially. Let it simmer until the juice has evaporated.

3   Add the shrimp mixture to rice and gently mix with a fork. Then place a paper towel over the pot and the lid over the paper towel. Reduce the heat to low and let it simmer for 10 minutes.

Serves 4.

Shrimp with Sun-Dried Tomatoes

1   In a bowl, place chopped sun-dried tomato and cover with 1 cup of boiling water. Let it sit for five minutes.

2   In a pot, heat oil and sauté onion until golden brown. Add garlic and shrimp to onion and sauté for a couple of minutes until the shrimp turns light orange. Add turmeric and cayenne pepper to onion mixture and sauté for a couple of minutes, then add mushrooms and continue to sauté.

3   Wash tomatoes and place them in a bowl. Cover with boiling water and let it sit for a couple of minutes. Then drain, remove the skin, and chop into small pieces.

4   Drain sun-dried tomato and mix with tomato paste and chopped tomato. Add this mixture to onion mixture and sauté. Add lemon juice and salt to onion mixture and cover the pot. Let it simmer for 10 minutes. Just before you serve, add chopped basil. You can serve this delicious dish over wild rice or organic pasta.

Serves 4.

1 lb.	cooked shrimp (peeled, deveined, tail off)
1	medium onion, chopped
2 cloves	garlic, chopped
½ cup	sun-dried tomato, chopped
1 cup	mushrooms, sliced
½ cup	fresh basil, chopped
2 cups	crushed tomato (4 medium tomatoes)
2 tbsp.	tomato paste
½ tsp.	sea salt
¼ tsp.	cayenne pepper
¼ tsp.	turmeric
4 tbsp.	olive oil
⅓ cup	fresh lemon, juiced

Stuffed Rainbow Trout

2 whole	rainbow trout (about 1 to 1 ½ lbs. of each)
2	fresh limes, juiced
½ cup	fresh dill, chopped (save 1 tbsp. for garnishing)
½ cup	cranberries, chopped
½ cup	bread crumbs
1	egg
1	onion, chopped
2 cloves	garlic, chopped
¼ cup	olive oil
½ tsp.	sea salt
½ tsp.	freshly grated pepper
Pinch	saffron

1 Cut a deep pocket on the body of trout from tail to the top fin. Empty the inside and wash and pat dry. Sprinkle inside and outside of trout with ¼ tsp. of salt and ¼ tsp. of pepper.

2 In a pot, heat 5 tbsp. of oil and sauté onion and garlic until golden brown. Add dill, cranberries, remaining salt and pepper, and saffron and sauté for a couple of minutes. Remove from the heat.

3 Beat the egg and mix with bread crumbs. Add it to onion mixture.

4 Stuff the fish with the onion mixture and close the opening with toothpicks. Mix lime juice and the remaining olive oil. Brush 1 side of the fish and then lay it down on a foil-lined, shallow baking pan. Brush the other side of the fish with the remaining lime and olive oil.

5 Preheat the oven to 350° F. and place the pan on the middle rack. Bake for 25 minutes. With a fork, test the flesh nearest the backbone; if it separates easily from the bone, it is done.

6 Transfer the fish gently to a serving dish and remove the foil and toothpicks. Garnish with chopped dill. You can serve this dish over basmati rice.

Serves 4.

Stuffed white Fish

1   With a sharp knife, make a cut from under the mouth all the way to the tail of the fish and clean inside, then wash and pat dry the fish. Use ¼ tsp. of salt and ¼ tsp. of pepper to rub all over the fish.

2   In a pot, heat 4 tbsp. of oil and sauté onion until golden brown. Rinse currants and add to onion. Sauté for a couple of minutes.

3   Add mint, tarragon, cilantro, pomegranate paste, walnut, and remaining salt and pepper to onion mixture and sauté for a couple of minutes.

4   In a bowl, mix garlic and lemon juice and set aside.

5   Fill the cavity of fish with onion mixture and close with toothpicks. Place aluminum foil over an oven dish, place the fish on top, and pour garlic mixture all over. Place the fish in the middle of the preheated 350° F. oven and cook for 20 to 25 minutes.

6   You can garnish this dish with parsley and lemon slices.

Serves 4.

1	white fish with head and tail on
½ cup	currants
1 cup	walnuts, chopped
⅓ cup each	fresh mint, tarragon, and cilantro, chopped
2	medium onions, chopped
1 clove	garlic, grated
1	lemon, sliced
1 tbsp.	parsley, chopped
½ tsp.	sea salt
½ tsp.	black pepper
½ cup	fresh lemon, juiced
¼ cup	vegetable oil
1 tsp.	pomegranate paste

White Fish Fillet with Ginger

2 lbs.	white fish fillet
1 cup	cilantro, chopped
1 clove	garlic, grated
1 tsp.	fresh ginger, grated
¼ tsp.	saffron
1 tbsp.	ginger, thinly sliced (for garnishing)
½ tsp.	turmeric
½ tsp.	black pepper, freshly grated
½ tsp.	sea salt
½ cup	lemon, juiced
½ cup	dates, chopped
½ cup	water
1 tbsp.	virgin olive oil

1 Preheat the oven to 350° F. Wash and pat dry fish fillet.

2 In a pot, bring water and dates to a boil, then reduce the heat and let it simmer until it becomes a paste.

3 In a bowl, mix cilantro, garlic, ginger, saffron, turmeric, salt, pepper, lemon juice, olive oil, and date paste.

4 Grease an oven dish with olive oil and place the fish fillet on the dish with skin side down.

5 Pour the mixture of cilantro all over the fillet and cover the dish with a sheet of foil. Place it in the refrigerator for 30 minutes.

6 After 30 minutes, remove the fish and place it in the middle of the oven and cook for 20 minutes.

7 You can garnish the fish with sliced fresh ginger.

Serves 4.

White Fish Patties

1   Wash fish fillet and pat dry, then sprinkle with salt and pepper. In a pot, place fillet with water on a medium heat, bring to a boil, then reduce the heat and let it simmer for 15 minutes.

2   In a bowl, grate onions and garlic. Beat the eggs and add to onion mixture.

3   In a bowl, flake the fillet with a fork and mix it with saffron, onion mixture, and bread crumbs.

4   In a pot, heat oil and use a measuring cup of (¼ cup of size) and fill the cup of with onion mixture. Pour into the pan and press with the back of a spoon. Continue with the rest and make sure you leave space between each of the patties.

5   Keep checking, and when 1 side is golden brown, turn the other side and let it cook. Place patties on a paper towel to catch the excess oil and then serve.

Serves 4.

2 lbs.	white fish fillet
3	eggs
2	medium onions
½ tsp.	sea salt
½ tsp.	black pepper
1 clove	garlic
¼ tsp.	saffron
1 cup	water
½ cup	bread crumbs
¼ cup	grape-seed oil

White Fish with Fig

2	white fish fillet
1 cup	dried figs, chopped
½ tsp.	ground cardamom
½ tsp.	cayenne pepper
½ tsp.	sea salt
½ cup	hazelnuts, chopped
1 cup	water
¼ cup	grape-seed oil
2 cups	fresh figs, sliced (for garnishing)

1 Wash fish fillet and pat dry. Preheat the oven to 350° F.

2 In a pot, mix chopped figs and water and bring to a boil, then reduce heat and add cardamom, cayenne pepper, and sea salt. Let it simmer until the liquid evaporates.

3 In a pot, roast chopped hazelnuts for 5 minutes, mixing constantly to avoid burning, and then set aside.

4 Place the fish fillet on a foil-lined, shallow baking pan and drizzle the grape-seed oil over the fillet. Pour the fig mixture all over; make sure the entire fillet is covered. Spread roasted hazelnuts on top, then cover with foil loosely.

5 Place the pan in the middle rack and bake for 20 to 25 minutes. Remove from the oven, garnish with fresh figs, and serve. You can serve this dish over couscous.

Serves 6.

Wild Salmon with Mint

1   Preheat oven to 350° F. Wash salmon fillet and pat dry.

2   In a pot, bring to a boil grated apple and apple juice, and then add lime juice, salt, and pepper. Reduce heat and let it simmer until it becomes thick. Add chopped mint and simmer for a couple of minutes. Remove from the heat and set aside.

3   Place the salmon fillet on a foil-lined, shallow baking pan and drizzle the grape-seed oil over. Pour apple mixture over the fillet; make sure it covers the entire fillet. Cover with foil.

4   Transfer the fillet into the oven and bake for 20 to 25 minutes on the middle rack.

5   You can serve this over quinoa or brown rice.

Serves 4.

2 lbs.	salmon fillet
1 cup	fresh mint, chopped
2 cups	golden delicious apple, grated
½ cup	lime, juiced
½ cup	grape-seed oil
½ tsp.	sea salt
¼ tsp.	chili pepper
½ cup	fresh apple, juiced

BAKED GOODS

Apple-Cinnamon Bread

2 cups	whole-wheat flour
2	eggs (save 1 tbsp. egg white for garnishing)
3	medium golden-delicious apples
2 tsp.	baking powder
2 tsp.	cinnamon powder (save ½ tsp. for garnishing)
1 cup	dates, chopped
1 cup	water
½ cup	grape-seed oil
1 ½ cups	raisin
½ cup	pistachios, slivered (save 1 tsp. pistachios for garnishing)

1 Preheat the oven to 350° F. and grease an 8 ½" round baking dish.

2 In a pot, bring chopped dates and water to a boil, reduce the heat, and let it simmer until the water evaporates and it becomes a paste.

3 Wash and peel apples. Thinly slice 1 and grate the other 2 with the large side of the grater.

4 In a bowl, beat the eggs well and then mix with oil, date paste, grated apple, and pistachios.

5 In a large bowl, mix flour, baking powder, cinnamon, and raisin. Combine flour mixture with egg mixture until smooth.

6 Pour in the greased baking dish, and arrange apple slices on top. Beat the egg white and brush the apple slices with egg white, and then sprinkle pistachios and cinnamon over the apples.

7 Bake the bread in the middle of the oven for 45 minutes or until the toothpick inserted in the center comes out clean.

8 Cool completely before slicing.

Banana-Nut Bread

1   Preheat oven to 350° F. and grease a round 9" pan.

2   In a pot, mix chopped dates and water and bring to a boil. Reduce heat and let it simmer until the water evaporates and it becomes a paste. Remove from the heat, and add ginger. Set aside to cool.

3   In a large bowl, mix flour, baking powder, baking soda, and chopped pecans.

4   In a bowl, mix mashed bananas, date paste, and oil. In another bowl, beat the eggs with an electric egg beater for a couple of minutes and add to banana mixture.

5   Mix banana and flour mixture and make sure they are well blended. Pour the batter into the greased pan, garnish with pecan halves, and bake in the middle of the oven for 30 minutes or until a toothpick inserted in the center comes out clean.

6   Remove from the oven and cool for 20 minutes. Cut into 8 pieces and serve.

2	very ripe bananas, mashed
1 cup	dates, chopped
1 cup	water
2	eggs
2 cups	whole-wheat flour
8	pecan halves
½ cup	grape-seed oil
½ tsp.	fresh ginger, grated
2 tsp.	baking powder
¼ tsp.	baking soda
½ cup	pecans, coarsely chopped

Banana-Raisin Bread

2	very ripe bananas
3 cups	whole-wheat flour
3 tsp.	baking powder
½ tsp.	baking soda
½ tsp.	cinnamon
⅓ cup	coconut oil
2	eggs
1 ½ cups	raisin
1 ½ cups	rice milk
1 ½ cups	pistachios, coarsely roasted chopped

1 Preheat the oven to 350° F. Grease a 9" x 5" x 3" loaf pan.

2 Mash bananas. Beat the egg with electric mixer and combine with oil and mashed bananas and rice milk.

3 In a large bowl, mix flour, baking powder, baking soda, and cinnamon. Combine the dry ingredients with egg mixture.

4 Fold in the raisin and pistachios.

5 Pour this batter into the greased pan and bake in the middle of the oven for 45 to 55 minutes. Check after 40 minutes by inserting a toothpick in the center; if it comes out clean, bread is baked. Otherwise, bake for another 10 minutes.

6 Remove from the oven and cool in the pan for 5 minutes, then unmold and cool on a rack for 20 minutes and serve.

Breakfast Coffee Bread

1 Preheat the oven to 350° F. Grease a 9" x 5" x 3" loaf pan with vegetable oil.

2 In a large bowl, mix flour, baking powder, baking soda, and cardamom seeds.

3 In a pot, bring chopped dates and water to a boil, reduce the heat, and let it simmer until the water evaporates and it becomes a paste.

4 In a bowl, beat the eggs for a couple of minutes, then add oil, milk, and date paste. Combine the egg mixture with flour mixture.

5 Add raisins and roasted almonds to egg mixture, making sure the batter is completely mixed.

6 Pour the batter into the loaf pan, brush with egg yolk, and garnish with sliced almonds. Bake in the middle of the oven for 35 to 40 minutes or until a toothpick inserted in the center comes out clean. Cool in the pan for 5 minutes, then unmold and cool on a rack for 20 minutes.

2 cups	whole-wheat flour
2 tsp.	baking powder
¼ tsp.	baking soda
2 cups	dates, chopped
1 ½ cup	water
1 tsp.	cardamom seeds
½ cup	grape-seed oil
2	eggs
1	egg yolk
¾ cup	almonds, slivered and roasted
½ cup	rice milk
¾ cup	raisins
½ cup	almonds, sliced

Cardamom & Date Bread

1 ½ cups	whole-wheat flour
1 cup	dates, chopped
1 cup	walnuts, chopped
2 tsp.	baking powder
½ tsp.	baking soda
½ cup	grape-seed oil
1 tsp.	cardamom seed, ground
2	eggs
1 cup	water
½ cup	rice milk

1 Preheat the oven to 325° F. and oil an 8" x 11" oven dish.

2 In a pot, bring water and chopped dates to a boil, then reduce the heat and let it simmer until the water evaporates and it becomes a paste. Set aside to cool.

3 In a bowl, beat the eggs with an electric mixer for a couple of minutes, then add date paste, oil, and milk to eggs and continue mixing.

4 In a bowl, combine flour, baking powder, baking soda, chopped walnuts, and cardamom.

5 Mix the egg and flour mixture and pour into the oven dish. Bake for 40 minutes in the middle of the oven. Check after 30 minutes by inserting a toothpick in the middle of the cake. If it comes out clean, the cake is ready. If not, bake for another 10 minutes. Cool in the pan for 5 minutes, then unmold and cool on a rack for 20 minutes.

Carrot-Raisin Bread

1   Preheat the oven to 350° F. Grease a 9" x 5" x 3" loaf pan.

2   In a large bowl, combine flour, clove, baking powder, baking soda, salt, nut, and raisins.

3   In a pot, bring chopped dates and water to a boil, and then reduce the heat and let it simmer until the water evaporates and it becomes a paste. Remove from the heat and let it cool.

4   In a bowl, beat the eggs with an electric mixer and then add date paste, oil, milk, lemon rind, cashew nuts, and carrots.

5   Add the dry ingredients to egg mixture and mix well. Pour the batter into the greased pan and bake in the middle of the oven for 35 to 45 minutes. Check after 35 minutes by inserting a toothpick in the center. If it comes out clean, remove the bread from the oven; otherwise, bake for another 10 minutes.

6   Cool it for 5 minutes inside the pan, and then remove the bread from the pan and place it on a wire rack to cool completely.

2 cups	carrots, grated
1 cup	dates, chopped
2 cups	whole-wheat flour
½ cup	raisins
2	eggs
½ cup	coconut oil
½ cup	cashew nuts, chopped
½ tsp.	lemon, rind
¼ tsp.	ground clove
2 tsp.	baking powder
¼ tsp.	baking soda
1 cup	water
½ cup	rice milk
Pinch	salt

Cinnamon Buns

2 ½ cups	whole-wheat flour
1 envelope	quick-rise instant yeast (8 g envelope)
¼ tsp.	sea salt
1 cup	basmati rice milk
½ cup	grape-seed oil
2	eggs
1 tbsp.	cinnamon
1 ½ cups	dates, chopped
1 cup	water
1 cup	raisins
½ cup	walnuts, chapped

1 Set aside ½ cup of whole-wheat flour from total amount. In a bowl, mix remaining flour, yeast, and salt.

2 In a pot, warm up milk and 5 tbsp. of the grape-seed oil, until hot. Stir hot liquids into the flour mixture.

3 In a bowl, beat the eggs and add to flour mixture. Mix the reserved flour a little bit at the time to egg mixture to make soft dough that does not stick to the bowl. (You might need the entire half cup of flour.) Turn onto a floured surface and knead for 10 minutes. Cover the dough with a towel and let it rest for 10 minutes.

4 In a pot, bring dates and water to a boil, then reduce heat and let it simmer until the water evaporates and it becomes a paste. Let it cool.

5 In a bowl, mix raisins, cinnamon, date paste, and the remaining grape-seed oil.

6 Roll dough into a 12" x 9" rectangle. Spread with cinnamon mixture, sprinkle with walnuts, and roll up from long side (jelly-rolls style). Then pinch to seal the seam.

7 Cut into equal slices with a sharp knife (12 pieces). Place cut sides up on a greased 9" x 13" oven dish, cover with a towel, and place the dish in the oven. Turn on the oven light **(not the oven)** and let the cinnamon buns rise in the warm oven for 30 minutes. After 30 minutes, remove the buns, preheat the oven to 350° F., and bake the cinnamon buns for 20 minutes. (You can serve them hot or cold.)

Date Cake

1 Preheat oven to 325° F. Grease 8" baking pan.

2 In a pot, bring dates and water to a boil, and then reduce the heat and let it simmer until the water evaporates and it becomes a paste. Remove from the heat and let it cool.

3 In a bowl, beat eggs for a couple of minutes, then add oil, date paste, ginger, and lemon peel. Mix well.

4 In another bowl, mix flour, baking powder, baking soda, hemp seed, and flaxseed. Stir this into the egg mixture until the dough is smooth, then add walnuts.

5 Pour the batter evenly in the pan and bake in the middle of the oven for 35 to 45 minutes. After 35 minutes, insert a toothpick in the center of the cake. If it comes out clean, the cake is ready; otherwise, bake for another 10 minutes.

6 Cool in the pan for 5 minutes, remove, and let it cool on a rack for 20 minutes. Then serve.

1 ½ cups	dates, chopped
1 ½ cup	whole-wheat flour
2 tsp.	baking powder
½ tsp.	baking soda
½ tsp.	fresh ginger, grated
½ cup	grape-seed oil
2	eggs
1 cup	water
1 cup	walnuts, chopped
2 tbsp.	hemp seed
1 tsp.	lemon peel, grated
1 tbsp.	flaxseed

Mango and Beet Cake

2 cups	whole-wheat flour
1 cup	fresh mango, juiced
1 cup	beet (cooked and grated)
1 cup	dates, chopped
1 cup	water
½ cup	grape-seed oil
2	eggs
2 tsp.	baking powder
½ tsp.	baking soda
⅛ tsp.	salt

1   Preheat the oven to 350° F.

2   Grease a 9" round cake pan, cover the base with wax paper, and grease the paper.

3   In a pot, bring dates and water into a boil, then reduce the heat and let it simmer until the water evaporates and it becomes a paste.

4   In a bowl, mix flour, baking powder, baking soda, and salt.

5   In a bowl, beat eggs with an electric mixer until it is thick and creamy, and then add oil, mango juice, grated beet, and the date paste to egg mixture. Fold in flour mixture and pour this batter into the prepared pan. Bake for 40 to 50 minutes.

6   Check after 35 minutes by inserting a toothpick in the center. If it comes out clean, remove it from the oven. Otherwise, bake for another 10 minutes.

7   Cool the cake for 5 minutes then remove from the pan and cool for 20 minutes.

Nut Bread

1. Preheat the oven to 350° F. Grease a 9" x 5" x 3" loaf pan.

2. In a pot, bring dates and water to a boil, reduce the heat, and let it simmer until the water evaporates and it becomes a paste. Remove from the heat and let it cool.

3. In a large bowl, mix flour, baking powder, baking soda, raisins, and the nuts.

4. In a bowl, beat the egg for a couple of minutes, then add date paste, oil, and rice milk to egg mixture and stir until it is blended. Add the flour mixture and mix well.

5. Pour this batter into the greased pan and bake in the middle of the oven for 40 to 50 minutes. Check after 40 minutes by inserting a toothpick in the center. If it comes out clean, remove from the oven. If not, continue baking for another 10 minutes. Cool in the pan for 5 minutes, then unmold and cool on a rack for 20 minutes.

2 cups	whole-wheat flour
1 cup	dates, chopped
1 cup	raisin
1 cup	water
2 tsp.	baking powder
½ tsp.	baking soda
½ cup	coconut oil
1	egg
1 ½ cups	rice milk
½ cup each	hazelnuts, almonds, and pistachios (chopped and roasted)

Orange-Beet Cake

2 cups	organic whole-wheat flour
1 cup	fresh beet, juiced
2 tbsp.	orange skin, grated
1 cup	beet (cooked and grated)
1 cup	dates, chopped
1 cup	water
½ cup	vegetable oil
3	eggs
2 tsp.	baking powder
½ tsp.	baking soda
½ tsp.	cardamom seeds, ground
¼ tsp.	salt

1 Grease an 8" baking pan, cover base with wax paper, and then grease the wax paper.

2 In a pot, bring dates and water to a boil, reduce the heat, and let it simmer until the water evaporates and it becomes a paste.

3 In a bowl, mix flour, cardamom seeds, baking powder, baking soda, and salt.

4 In a bowl, beat eggs with electric mixer until thick and creamy, and then add oil, beet juice, orange skin, beets, and date paste to egg mixture.

5 Combine flour mixture with egg mixture and pour the batter into prepared pan. Bake in a preheated 350° F. oven for 35 to 45 minutes.

6 Insert a toothpick in the center after 40 minutes. If it comes out clean, the cake is ready. If not, bake for another 5 minutes.

7 Remove from the oven and let it sit for 5 minutes. Remove from the pan and let it cool on a rack for 20 minutes.

Orange-Date Bread

1 Preheat the oven to 350° F. Grease a 9" x 11" oven dish.

2 In a pot, bring the chopped dates and water to a boil, then reduce heat and let it simmer until the water evaporates and it becomes a paste. Set aside to cool.

3 In a bowl, mix flour, baking powder, baking soda, pecan, and cinnamon.

4 In another bowl, beat the eggs for a couple of minutes and then add oil, date paste, orange peel, and orange juice to egg mixture.

5 Mix the flour mixture and egg mixture with a wooden spoon.

6 Pour the batter into the oven dish and place it in the middle of the oven. Bake for 35 to 40 minutes.

7 Check after 30 minutes by inserting a toothpick in the center of the bread. If it comes out clean, then the bread is ready. If not, bake for another 5 to 10 minutes.

8 Cool for 20 minutes before serving.

1 cup	dates, pitted and chopped
2 cups	whole-wheat flour
2 tsp.	baking powder
½ tsp.	baking soda
½ cup	vegetable oil
2	eggs
1 cup	fresh orange, juiced
1 cup	water
1 cup	pecans, coarsely chopped
1 tbsp.	orange peel, grated
1 tsp.	cinnamon

Pecan and Cinnamon Biscotti

2 cups	whole-wheat flour
2 tsp.	baking powder
½ tsp.	baking soda
2 tsp.	cinnamon
1 cup	dates, chopped
2	eggs
½ cup	raisins
½ cup	pecan halves
1 cup	water
½ cup	rice milk
½ cup	vegetable oil

1   Preheat the oven to 350° F. Grease a baking sheet with vegetable oil.

2   In a bowl, mix flour, baking powder, baking soda, cinnamon, raisins, and pecans.

3   In a pot, bring chopped dates and water to a boil, then reduce heat and let it simmer until the water evaporates and it becomes a paste. Set aside to cool.

4   In a bowl, beat eggs, and then add date paste, rice milk, and oil to egg mixture and mix well.

5   Add flour mixture to egg mixture and use your hands to mix. Then transfer the dough on a lightly floured surface and roll into a loaf about 14" x 4". Place the loaf on a baking sheet and bake for 25 to 30 minutes until it is firm to touch. Remove from the oven and let it cool for 10 minutes on an oven rack.

6   Cut the log diagonally into ½ inch thickness with a serrated knife and place each slice sideways on the baking sheet. Then bake for 5 minutes, and turn each slice over to bake for another 5 minutes.

7   You can serve these healthy and delicious biscotti with tea or coffee.

Pistachio Biscotti

1 Preheat the oven to 325° F. Grease a baking sheet.

2 In a pot, bring chopped dates and water to a boil, then reduce heat and let it simmer until the water has evaporated and it becomes a paste. Set aside to cool.

3 In a bowl, mix flour, baking powder, sesame seed, and pistachios.

4 In another bowl, beat the eggs and oil together until smooth. Then add date paste and vanilla to egg mixture. Mix flour mixture with egg mixture, and make 2 small loaves about a foot long and 1 ½" wide on a lightly floured surface.

5 Place loaves 2" apart on the baking sheet, then place the baking sheet in the middle of the oven and bake for 25 minutes. Remove loaves and let it cool completely.

6 Cut each loaf into 12 slices diagonally with a serrated knife, and place each slice on its side on the baking sheet. Bake for another 5 minutes, and turn each slice to other side and bake until golden brown. Let it cool and serve.

2 cups	whole-wheat flour
1 cup	pistachios (chopped and roasted)
1 cup	dates, chopped
2	eggs
½ cup	grape-seed oil
1 tsp.	vanilla
2 tsp.	baking powder
2 tbsp.	sesame seed, roasted
1 cup	water

Raspberry-Hazelnut Bread

2 cups	whole-wheat flour
2	eggs
1 cup	fresh raspberries, juiced
1 cup	dates, chopped
1 cup	water
1 cup	hazelnuts (roasted and chopped)
½ cup	grape-seed oil
2 tsp.	baking powder
½ tsp.	baking soda

Sauce

1 cup	raspberry juice
1 cup	grape juice
½ cup	dates, chopped
1 tbsp.	rosewater

1 Preheat the oven to 350° F. Grease an 8 ½" x 4 ½" x 2 ½" loaf pan. In a bowl, mix flour, baking powder, and baking soda together.

2 In a pot, bring dates and water to a boil, then reduce the heat and let it simmer until the water has evaporated and it becomes a paste. Set aside to cool.

3 In a bowl, beat the eggs with and electric mixer until thick and creamy and then add oil, raspberry juice, date paste, and hazelnuts to egg mixture. Add flour mixture to the egg mixture and pour the batter into the greased pan. Bake in the middle of the oven for 35 to 45 minutes. Check after 35 minutes by inserting a toothpick in the center. If it comes out clean, remove from the oven; otherwise, bake for another 10 minutes.

4 For the sauce, bring raspberries, grape juice, chopped dates, to a boil. Reduce the heat and let it simmer for 10 minutes. Add rosewater and then remove from the heat and let it cool. Use this sauce over your bread and serve.

Rolled Oat and Raisin Cookies

1   In a bowl, mash banana. Beat the egg with an electric mixer and then add to mashed banana. Add peanut butter, rolled oats, raisins, and vanilla to egg mixture.

2   Preheat the oven to 325° F. and grease a cookie tray.

3   With a spoon, place the batter one spoon at a time onto the tray making sure there is enough space between each cookie, to avoid sticking together.

4   Place the tray in the middle rack of the oven and bake for 10 minutes or until light golden.

5   Remove the tray from the oven and let the cookies cool and then serve.

Makes 12

¼ cup	peanut butter
1	ripe banana
1 cup	rolled oats
½ cup	raisin
1	egg
½ tsp.	vanilla

Rose-Water Coconut Squares

1 cup	dates, chopped
1 cup	water
1 ¼ cups	unsweetened coconut, roasted
2	eggs
1 cup	whole-wheat flour
1 tsp.	baking powder
½ tsp.	baking soda
4 tbsp.	rose water
½ cup	vegetable oil

1 Preheat the oven to 350° F. Grease a 9" x 11" baking dish.

2 In a pot, bring water and dates to a boil, and then reduce the heat and let it simmer until the water has evaporated and it becomes a paste. Set aside to cool.

3 In a bowl, mix flour, baking powder, and baking soda together.

4 In another bowl, beat eggs with an electric mixer. Add oil, rose water, and date paste to egg mixture and continue mixing.

5 Combine 1 cup of coconut to flour mixture and add this to egg mixture. Pour this batter into the baking dish. Sprinkle ¼ cup of coconut on top and bake in the middle of the oven for 20 to 30 minutes. Check by inserting a toothpick in the center. If toothpick does not come out clean, cook for another 5 minutes. Cool completely and cut into 24 small squares.

Strawberry and Date Bread

1 Preheat the oven to 350° F. Grease an 8" round cake pan, cover base with wax paper, and grease the wax paper.

2 In a pot, bring dates and water to a boil, then reduce the heat and let it simmer until the water has evaporated and it becomes a paste. Remove from heat and let it cool.

3 In a bowl, beat eggs with an electric mixer until thick and creamy. Then add oil, date paste, strawberries, lemon rind, rice milk, and vanilla to egg mixture.

4 In another bowl, mix flour, baking soda, and baking powder together, and gradually stir in the egg mixture and mix well. Pour the batter into the greased pan and bake in the middle of the oven for 35 minutes. Check to see if it is done by inserting a toothpick in the center after 35 minutes. If it comes out clean, the bread is baked; otherwise, bake for another 10 minutes. Cool completely and then serve.

2 cups	strawberries, chopped
1 cup	dates, chopped
2 cups	whole-wheat flour
2 tsp.	baking powder
½ tsp.	baking soda
2	eggs
½ cup	vegetable oil
½ cup	rice milk
1 tsp.	lemon, rind
1 cup	water

Triple Berry Coffee Bread

2 cups	combined blackberries, raspberries, and blueberries
2	eggs
1 cup	strawberries, sliced (for garnishing)
½ cup	grape-seed oil
¼ tsp.	vanilla
2 tbsp.	cocoa powder
1 cup	dates, chopped
2 cups	whole-wheat flour
2 tsp.	baking powder
½ tsp.	baking soda
1 cup	water

1   Preheat the oven to 350° F. Grease an 8" round cake pan. Cut a round shape out of wax paper and place it at the bottom of the cake pan. Grease the wax paper.

2   In a pot, bring water and dates into a boil. Then reduce the heat and let it simmer until the water evaporates and it becomes a paste.

3   In a bowl, beat the egg and then add the date paste, oil, and vanilla to the egg mixture. Mix berries with the egg mixture.

4   In another bowl, mix flour, baking powder, baking soda, and cocoa powder together. Pour in the egg mixture a little at a time and mix gently. Pour the batter into a greased pan and cook for 35 to 45 minutes in the middle of the oven. Before removing from the oven, insert a toothpick in the center of the bread. If it comes out clean, the bread is baked. If not, bake for another 5 to 10 minutes.

5   Remove from the oven and let it cool, then you can garnish it with sliced strawberries.

Zucchini Bread

1   Preheat the oven to 350° F. Grease 2 different 9" x 5" loaf pans.

2   In a pot, bring dates and water to a boil, then reduce the heat and let it simmer until the water evaporates and it becomes a paste. Set aside to cool.

3   In a bowl, beat the eggs and then add oil, date paste, grated lemon skin, apple, and zucchini.

4   In another bowl, mix flour, baking powder, baking soda, and almonds, and add this to the egg mixture. Divide the batter equally in 2 loaves and pour into greased pans.

5   Bake in the middle of the oven for 50 to 60 minutes. Check after 45 minutes by inserting a toothpick in the center. If it does not come out clean, continue to bake for another 10 minutes, until the toothpick comes out clean. Cool for 10 minutes, then remove from the pan and let it cool completely on a wire rack.

3 cups	whole-wheat flour
1 cup	dates, chopped
2 cups	zucchini, grated
1 cup	golden delicious apple, grated
1 cup	water
3	eggs
1 cup	almonds (chopped and roasted)
½ cup	grape-seed oil
1 tsp.	lemon skin, grated
2 tsp.	baking powder
½ tsp.	baking soda

Index